SEA MAGIC

Fidelio Photography

About the Author

Sandra Kynes describes herself as an explorer: she likes finding underlying similarities and connections in our world, then crafting new ways to interact with them. Looking at things a little differently has resulted in six books thus far. Her curiosity has taken her on many travels and to live in New York City, Europe, England, and New England. In addition to studying ancient texts such as *The Mabinogion*, Celtic history, myth, and magic, she has explored a range of spiritual practices. Sandra is a yoga instructor, massage therapist, and Reiki practitioner.

Sea Magic

Connecting with the *Ocean's Energy*

Sandra Kynes

Llewellyn Publications
Woodbury, Minnesota

Cover design by Ellen Dahl

Cover illustration © Wen Hsu

Interior book design by Joanna Willis

Interior illustrations by Wen Hsu, except pages 69, 145, 148, and 172 by Llewellyn art department

Llewellyn is a registered trademark of Llewellyn Worldwide, Ltd.

ISBN 978-0-7387-1353-3

Llewellyn Publications
A Division of Llewellyn Worldwide, Ltd.

Printed in the United States of America

This book is dedicated to the memory of **Rachel Carson**—a brilliant scientist who never lost her sense of awe for the ocean.

CONTENTS

*W*hen the soul has been wounded and the sun is keen
to surface in the dark there is one place I go to,
that place that fills the earth's land with moisture and
water, that changes the coast in a dream, that place
the ancients call mother of mothers, the ocean . . .

JOHN PULE
Ocean Song to Myself

INTRODUCTION

When I was a child, my family spent part of each summer on the Delaware coast in a cottage that stood one block from the ocean and one block from the bay. There was always entertainment on the bay, where interesting boats docked along a rickety network of gangways and piers, but it was the ocean that held sway over my attention. It provided endless fun and fascination, and at night its soothing rhythm was a background lullabye that calmed the excitement of the day.

When I was very small, the crashing surf intimidated me, but once I had the gumption to venture in without holding my mother's hand, the sea worked its magic on me. Even then, the ocean's push and pull seemed like more than just a fun kiddie ride. I felt its mystery, power, and beauty on a level that I didn't understand at the time.

The little gifts that the sea yielded carried a sense of awe for me. Back home, I spent hours in my bedroom arranging the shells and other found objects I had toted home in my suitcase. Somehow these were more than just a collection of vacation memorabilia. In hindsight, I see that I viewed these little treasures as sacred—they were not toys. I sensed something unique about each seashell, and having them all over my room made me feel that I was communing with something special. Like the tides, my collection of shells ebbed and flowed, but it was an interest that I took into adulthood.

Despite those childhood summers by the shore, I did not become a beach person as I grew up. I didn't feel compelled to recapture the summer seaside experience; instead, I was drawn to the shore during the off season. Without the warm-weather crowds and noise I could find that special connection again.

But then, of course, in my adulthood, life happened: a job, raising a child. Many years passed before I returned to the sea, but it was never completely absent from my life. In the 1980s, I escaped the dullness of an uninteresting job in Manhattan by spending my lunch hours in a wonderful old shop filled with seaside treasures. Discovering the store was like finding a magical secret garden where I could step outside the bustling world of New York City and into a place where time wasn't important. Veronica, the shop's marvelous owner, answered all my questions and shared her knowledge as I browsed amongst the shelves and cabinets that were chock-full of every imaginable type of shell. Years later I learned that she was Veronica Parker Johns, a mystery writer who also happened to be the grande dame of conchology in the New York area. Despite my relocating a number of times since then—including overseas—I still have most of the shells I bought from her. A few of them have suffered more wear and tear from my cats than from the ocean.

After what seemed like a lifetime removed from those days in New York, the running waves along Castlemaine Harbor in Ireland heralded my return to a sea consciousness. I was on pilgrimage with my senses wide open, ready to receive whatever I was meant to observe and learn. Deep in my bones I could feel the power of my ancestral land washed and purified by the sea that surrounded it. I realized how the intricate interactions of the three permanent elements of earth, air, and water touch and shape the human psyche.

The sea has always been a place of mystery, its vastness beautiful, awesome, and fearsome. It is teeming with creatures so different from land dwellers that it seemed worthy of the warning on old maps: "Here be monsters." The ocean was mysterious, and it was believed to conceal the Isles of the Otherworld, the places of magic and spirit. A few Celtic heroes managed to journey there and back again—but they were always changed. Sea change—transformation.

While it took a long time for this book to come into being, its real birth manifested on a rugged Maine shore when my family and I were house-hunting for our return to New England. I realized that something about the sea allows adults to feel like children and play in the water and sand. The beach is a place where we can just be (*be*ach), and it is when we reach this state of being that we can find who we truly are. When we come to this source we can activate the magic within us and connect fully with the power of the natural world.

The ocean helps us listen to the voice of our souls. We need to hear this wisdom and connect with our inner self, but we also need our outer everyday self because it knows how to operate in the physical world. Eckhart Tolle has expressed these two selves as the mind (thinking) and being (consciousness). He said that "the mind is essentially a survival ma-chine . . . gathering, storing and analyzing information."[1] But being "is a state of connectedness with something immeasurable" that is "essentially you and yet is much greater than you. It is finding your true nature be-yond name and form."[2] All too often the inner self is not heard amidst the noise with which we surround ourselves. In Tolle's words, "this incessant mental noise prevents you from finding that realm of inner stillness that is inseparable from being."[3]

Just as the ocean has been a vast uncharted wilderness until relatively recent times, it has also remained fairly untapped for energy work and in-ner path exploration. The sea offers us many tools for accessing that realm of inner stillness and wisdom that resides at the core of our souls. It beck-ons us to search and discover the reason for our being on this earth in this time and this place.

I've come to think that my given name was no accident. During my childhood I was called Sandy (although only my mother gets away with that now). Sometimes I was teased: I would hear my name called and when I responded, the reply was "Sandy beach!" It wasn't amusing at the time, but I have come to feel the connection.

---

1 Eckhart Tolle, *The Power of Now*, 19.

2 Ibid., 10.

3 Ibid., 12.

Being a water sign, too, aids in my role as a guide to the *beach*; to that wonderful in-between place blessed by Mother Ocean where we can feel the power of her embrace. Metaphorically, we step from the beach into the true currents of our lives. Here, awash in the natural world, we discover our own sacred balance. Whether you live inland or near the coast, this book will help you stroll Mother Ocean's beach with your heart and soul, exploring the beauty and wisdom that await you.

I

THE CALL OF THE OCEAN

These are the tests of the sea:
The third wave is for courage,
The sixth wave is for perseverance,
The ninth wave is for surrender.

LUNAEA WEATHERSTONE
Celtic Mandala Journal

MANY PEOPLE TODAY DEPEND ON the sea for their food and livelihood, just as humans have done for millennia. Indeed, the ocean provided sustenance long before the development of agriculture and the rise of civilization. Communities have always clustered on the earth's coastlines, and on the waterways that flow to them. The sea is our true source.

For a time the people of antiquity believed that "the great ocean was thought to be unnavigable, flowing around the world like a river," in the words of Fletcher Bassett.[1] This concept lived on in later Norse mythology. Even though the ocean separates the continents, it also serves as a highway to unite people. Venturing out to sea and developing navigational skills brought increased contact among ancient civilizations—a catalyst for the spread of Neolithic culture around 8000 BCE.[2]

Many of these early people worshipped a mother goddess whose many roles included nurturing and sustenance. The names of some of these goddesses, and of the saints who came later, were derived from the sea: Mara, Maia, Mary, Maria, Marian, and Miriam.[3] The Latin root word, *mare*, means "sea." In French *la mère* means "mother" and *la mer* means "sea."[4]

The goddesses known as Aphrodite, Ishtar, and Venus were called Stella Maris, or Star of the Sea. This title was also given to the Virgin Mary, who was usually depicted in a flowing blue cloak and white dress, "the

---

1 Fletcher Bassett, *Legends and Superstitions of the Sea and of Sailors*, 12.

2 Marija Gimbutas, *The Civilization of the Goddess*, 4.

3 Anna Franklin, *The Illustrated Encyclopedia of Fairies*, 227.

4 Jules Cashford, *The Moon: Myth and Image*, 80.

colors of wave and foam."[5] It was no accident that people of the Mediterranean viewed Mary, too, as a goddess of the sea: she was beautiful, nurturing, mysterious, divine.

In addition to finding a source of food, people have been drawn by the sea's mesmerizing sight and sound; something primal in that endless rhythm calls to us. Author Don Groves noted that we have an "atavistic at-homeness" with the sea.[6] It is unimaginably vast and at times terrifyingly wild, yet something beckons to us and we know we are tied to the ocean. It's no wonder that the primordial seas were central to many creation myths—a topic we will turn to later in this book.

Life began in the sea, and three-quarters of our body's fluids are biochemically similar to seawater.[7] Individually, we begin life in the ocean of our mothers' wombs, floating in amniotic fluid with a chemical composition similar to seawater. We develop in stages not unlike the evolution "from gill-breathing inhabitants of water"[8] to land creatures that breathe air.

What is the relevance of our evolutionary past for us today? Even if we wanted to, we could not turn back the clock and return to that floating state of comfort and safety. But we can rediscover a primal rhythm within us; we can find our center and our balance in a chaotic world. Finding our life-affirming watery center gives us a place from which we can grow as individuals. Like running waves, we can develop our energy to enhance our own lives as well as those around us. The vast power of the ocean is available to support us in these personal endeavors.

---

5 Diana Ferguson, *The Magickal Year*, 97.

6 Don Groves, *The Oceans*, viii.

7 Ibid., vii.

8 Rachel Carson, *The Sea Around Us*, 18.

What Is Magic?

Magic is an attitude toward the world and an awareness of its natural rhythms. It's a way of perceiving and living in the world. It's the small occurrences that remind us who we are and where we, as individuals, fit into the vast web of life. Magic has much to do with our connection to the natural world. For example, trees are living entities and when we open our spirits to their energy we can sense a living connection that adds a new dimension to how we perceive our neighborhoods and the places we visit.

To me, coincidence is another form of magic—one that can occur as a major life event or as a minor incident that might even go unnoticed. Either way, it usually shepherds us toward or away from something or someone. Coincidence is a guiding hand that provides a gentle nudge or sometimes a shove to get us on the right track.

And then there's magic in the form of energy that we raise through prayer, meditation, or ritual to manifest our intentions into the physical realm. While these forms of magic seem very different from one another, they are interconnected in a way that helps integrate our spiritual and everyday lives. We feel less dichotomy between our inner self and outer self; we feel more whole, less fragmented.

Discovering the Sea's Magic

Water is symbolically associated with emotion, with inner flowing. Water is formless and yet forming. It represents transformation; we sometimes refer to this process as a sea change. The sea is a great icon for ongoing change because its own constant shifting also endlessly changes the shoreline.

The sea is mysterious; its primal call draws us and holds us spellbound. Its energy speaks to us on a level where we don't often venture, distracted as we are by our culture's superficial, materialistic ideals. However, the more we are swept into the shoals of banality, the more we lose touch with the depth of our souls, those we love, and the natural world around us. Physically we may live in riches but spiritually we are poverty stricken.

We are left hungering to find out who we are and where we belong in this world. The sea can bring us back to that state of grace where we feel awed by the beauty of life and are humbled, grateful to be part of it. The sea can help us explore self, define our inner path and lead us out into the world knowing that we each have our unique place. By allowing nature to have a hand in shaping us we can stop our haphazard chasing from one thing to another and focus on the meaningful aspects of our lives.

The beach, that ever-changing overlapping place of earth and sea, is a metaphor for those of us who are seekers. Like the beach, we are in-between, mentally and emotionally, as we search for meaning in our lives.

What happens when we land dwellers connect with Mother Ocean?

- We honor our primordial source.

- We connect with the nurturing of the natural world—food, beauty, solace.

- We tap into one of the greatest powers on this planet.

- We acknowledge the largest portion of this earth—after all, we live on the "big blue marble," the planet that is 70 percent water.

Sea Magic—working with the energy of the ocean—serves to deepen our experience as we journey through life. Whether you live near the ocean or just visit the shore occasionally, using the suggestions in this book while at the beach can be a powerful and moving experience.

With a little research you may even find that you live in an area that was once an ancient ocean. In ages past, the sea crept over the land and receded many times as violent earthquakes and volcanoes shaped and reshaped the continents. One common sign of an ancient sea is limestone, a sedimentary rock that contains the calicified remains of marine life. The North American inland sea of 265 to 440 million years ago left abundant traces in the form of limestone in places such as Mammoth Cave, Kentucky. Over two thousand years ago in what is now Britain, ancient people left their mark on chalky hillsides where the soil is still infused with the shells of tiny sea creatures and calcium carbonate.[9] They selectively removed soil and grass to create enormous, beautiful sacred images. One gleaming example is the White Horse of Uffington, high on an escarpment of the Berkshire Downs in what is now Oxfordshire. Its flowing lines seem to undulate with the topography of the hillside and can be seen for miles around. Limestone outcrops have even been found at 20,000 feet above sea level in the Himalayas.[10]

While traces of ancient seas can be found in the most unusual places, the real beauty of Sea Magic is that you do not need to be near the ocean—ancient or otherwise—to use it. Because of our primal connection with the sea, we can invoke its power from within ourselves. After all, water is the element related to the inner self. The energy of magic emanates from the depths of our being. Memory and imagination serve as powerful tools to create and re-create experiences.

Using Sea Magic and drawing closer to the oceanic realm also raises our awareness of the interconnectedness and fragility of our world. Let us be mindful that gifts from the sea come with the responsibility of protecting the oceans. It is our duty to live in awareness; to cease further harm to the ocean, and to aid in cleaning it up in any way we can. For ideas, see "Health: Ours and the Ocean's" in section VI of this book. Through our daily choices, we can promote health on both these levels. It's not that hard. You don't have to quit your job and become an environmental crusader to make a difference.

Sea Magic is a path for being and living in the world whether you are near or far from the coast. This book will give you new knowledge of the sea's wonders. You will also learn some simple practices that will deepen your connection with yourself—through the ocean. Although many of the practices presented here are spiritual in nature, they are intended to support your religious orientation, not replace it. Sea Magic can amplify your current meditative practices, or it can help you get started. The real magic occurs when you make it your own by adding personal nuances that hold meaning for you. Explore, and Mother Ocean will reward you.

---

9 Ibid., 83.
10 Ibid.

JOURNALING: EXPLORING CHANGE

We often live in such a blur of activity that many of the once-important milestones of our lives fall by the wayside and are forgotten. The popular art of scrapbooking is one way to preserve memories of external events, but what about the internal ones? It's easy to forget how far we have come along our inner paths. The ability to look back can be a powerful tool for bringing the present into focus and furthering our journey.

Keeping a journal lets us explore ourselves through writing. This kind of journaling is not to be confused with the "Dear Diary, Today I . . ." writings of our preteen years. Here, there are no hard and fast rules except honesty. (If we're dishonest in our journal, do we think we can fool ourselves?) Journal entries do not have to be written every day, week, month, or year, for that matter. My journals date back more than thirty years, and there are some gaps of a year or more. But journaling is something I return to time and again. In times of change, the act of writing helps me sort things out, and looking back on my journal later gives me valuable perspective. In hindsight, so much makes sense, and I can piece things together: feelings, thoughts, events. Many "aha" moments occur. Journaling is especially important when we are going through periods of change. It may not be until much later when we reread what we've written that the light bulb of self-discovery goes on.

Because we are connecting with the ocean's energy—which has a way of slowing us down for reflection—I encourage you to start (or continue) a journal as you read this book. When I traveled to Ireland three years ago, I kept a journal before, during, and for a time after my pilgrimage. Whenever I reread those pages I find clarity for the present. I keep my current journal on my bedside table so I can record dreams before they disappear. Like dreams, things that occur during meditation, journeying, and energy work can vanish in a split second like a wisp of smoke. Capturing them on the spot can bring guidance to our inner soul path. As you follow the practices in this book, you may want to keep your journal at hand to record your experiences and thoughts.

Each section of this book ends with a few questions to use as starting points for your journaling sessions. The questions don't have to be addressed all at once, in any particular order, or at all. You need not write only complete, well-thought-out sentences; getting your feelings and thoughts on paper is the point. If some questions spark other thoughts, follow each to see where it takes you.

Similarly, a technique called mind mapping can aid in bringing thoughts to the surface by word association, as explained in appendix A. This technique helps us let go of linear thinking and move our thought flow in many directions. This may seem fragmenting at first, but when you've taken it as far as you can, and then look at the whole picture, you'll finding interesting interconnections that you might otherwise overlook.

As you progress through this book, keeping a journal can enhance your experience and provide another avenue of approach for working your inner path.

GETTING TO KNOW THE OCEAN

When I bought a used copy of Don Groves' book *The Oceans*, I found an inscription at the front, from a father to his son: "Most of the world is here—we should understand it." This is vitally important advice for our everyday experience in the world. And I believe it is especially relevant for those of us who are seekers, who want to know more about ourselves, the natural world, and the mysteries that enfold it all.

As you embark on this journey into Sea Magic, ask yourself what you already know about the world's oceans. Okay, they're big and they usually appear to be some shade of blue or blue-green. Like most of us, unless your education or profession is connected with the sea, you might not know very much about it. So let's take a brief "natural history tour" of the ocean. How did it originate? What do its shifting colors mean? What creates waves? (We will discuss tides and the moon later, in section VI.)

In the beginning—well, not the very beginning—the new earth was wrapped in a dense layer of cloud. The cooling and cracking of the earth's surface in response to internal strain and pressure created the continents and the deep valleys in between. Rain fell on the planet continuously, but much of it evaporated. As the earth continued to cool, the evaporation slowed, and the great empty basins and hollows began to fill with water. Minerals were leached from rock, leaving behind salt which also eventually washed into the forming oceans. (This process is still occurring some two billion years later.) The salty soup of molecules in that dimly-lit and hot environment produced the cauldron from which an "endless stream of life" would emerge.[11]

Even though we tend to think in terms of separate oceans—Atlantic, Pacific and so on—there is really only one world ocean. This interconnecting body of water covers some 142 million square miles.[12] Although most of us tend to use the words *ocean* and *sea* interchangeably (as is the case in this book), there is a difference. An ocean is part of the global body of water, whereas a sea can also mean a landlocked body of saltwater. For example, the Dead Sea and the Caspian Sea do not connect with the global ocean, but the Mediterranean Sea does.

As for mystery, the deep ocean is as alien to us as outer space. Where sunlight does not penetrate, sea animals create their own luminescence in the dark waters. As a child I stared at pictures of these strange creatures in an encyclopedia, trying to convince my young mind that these were not some invention of the Brothers Grimm.

As for color, the way our eyes perceive light determines how we see the ocean's waters. Refracted light produces a wide range of changeable sea colors—the greens of the coastal areas and the deep blues of the open sea. Why is blue predominant? Sunlight bouncing off water molecules reflects a high percentage of blue rays back to our eyes. In deep water, red and yellow rays of the color spectrum get absorbed, resulting in mostly blue reflecting back. But in coastal areas, algae, microorganisms, and minerals play a role in the absorption and reflection of light, producing an endless variety of hues. Some notable examples are the Red Sea and, in many of the earth's waters, the occasional red tides caused by an overabundance of red algae.

---

11 Ibid., 12.

12 Groves, *Oceans*, 18.

CURRENTS AND WAVES

Currents can be thought of as rivers within the ocean. Some flow only a few feet under the surface while others move far below in the depths. The Gulf Stream, running from the east coast of the United States to the Atlantic north of Scotland, may be the most well-known current, but it is only one of many.

Ocean currents are caused by a combination of factors: the earth's rotation, winds, differences in water density and temperature, and the shape of the underwater landscape. For the most part, currents move in that sacred pattern found throughout nature—the spiral. In the Northern Hemisphere they move clockwise and in the Southern they move counterclockwise, resulting in a global cauldron of balanced energy.

Perhaps most fascinating are the waves—the ceaseless rolling across open seas, and the breakers that wash the shore and create that betwixt-and-between mixture of land and water. Coastal dwellers who are in tune with nature learn how to read waves. Pacific Islanders know that certain types of waves indicate that a typhoon is on its way. In the aftermath of the December 2004 tsunami, news reports noted that tribal people on remote Indonesian islands saw the signs and headed for high ground, which saved their lives.[13]

Waves move in groups called "wave trains," frequently in threes.[14] The last wave of a train is said to be the most powerful. To Celtic people, the ninth wave (third wave of the third group—triple triad) was a symbolically significant barrier. A Welsh sea poem tells of the dead being buried "where the ninth wave breaks."[15]

To be banished beyond the ninth wave meant you were an outcast. Beyond this point, however, high adventure began. This marked the magical boundary of the Otherworld. Beyond the ninth wave one had to rely on the power of wisdom, the power of ancestors, and the power of soul.

---

13 Neelesh Misra and Rupak Sanyal, *Ancient Tribe Survives Tsunami*, Associated Press, Jan. 6, 2005, www.cbsnews.com/stories/2005/01/04/world/main664729.shtml.

14 Carson, *Sea Around Us*, 91.

15 Bassett, *Legends and Superstitions*, 26.

In Irish myth, the Tuatha de Danann requested time to prepare for battle
and asked the Milesians to "withdraw the length of nine waves from the
shore and then return."[16] With their foes at the magical boundary, the
Danann were able to raise a mist that hid Ireland—at least temporarily.

PRACTICE: NINEFOLD SEA BLESSING

In more recent times, the people of Ireland and Scotland have used a ninefold blessing of water asking the sea to impart good qualities to an infant.[17]
If you are ready to step into the practice of Sea Magic, this is a nice gesture
with which to begin your journey. The Ninefold Sea Blessing is slightly
reworded here to fit our purposes. You can simply read it to yourself, or if
you prefer a more formal entry, make a personal ritual of it.

First, prepare some saltwater. Collect a little ocean water if you can or
create it by dissolving a large pinch of sea salt into a small jar of warm
spring water. (Avoid using tap water as it contains fluoride and other
chemicals; water for a blessing should be as pure as possible.) When the
salt has dissolved, hold the jar in both hands in front of your heart as
you speak the words of the Seawater Preparation.

When you are finished, close your eyes. Continue to hold the jar at your
heart and visualize the ocean. With your hands, feel the sea's energy emanating from the jar. When the feeling is strong, open your eyes. Your seawater is ready to use.

Seawater Preparation

"Mother Ocean, from whom life flows,
bless this water with your love and nurturing power,
your endless beauty and strength.
For this I am grateful.
Blessed be."

---

16 T. W. Rolleston, *Celtic Myths and Legends*, 135.

17 Caitlin and John Matthews, *Encyclopedia of Celtic Wisdom*, 235.

Now place a blue or other sea-colored cloth on your meditation altar or a table. A seashell such as a scallop or clam or even a shell-shaped dish can be used as a vessel for the seawater.

Take a few minutes to quiet your mind, then think about the words of Lunaea Weatherstone at the beginning of this section: "These are the tests of the sea: The third wave is for courage, the sixth wave is for perseverance, the ninth wave is for surrender." Becoming a seeker and wanting to go beyond our everyday experiences takes courage. Once we begin to tread the inner path, it takes perseverance to stay the course. At the point where we uncover truth, we have a choice: we can go back to what we know, or we can trust our intuition—our inner knowing— and surrender its wisdom, letting the journey unfold.

When you are ready, read the Ninefold Sea Blessing. After you speak each line, dip a finger into the seawater and then touch the top of your head. This is your crown chakra, your energy center of spirit.

Ninefold Sea Blessing

"A small wave for my smile,
A small wave for my voice,
A small wave for my laughter,
A small wave for my choice.
A small wave for my sight,
A small wave for my wealth,
A small wave for my generosity,
A small wave for my health.
A small wave for my truth;
Mother Ocean, I ask for nine waves of grace upon me."

When you are finished, close your eyes. Sit for a minute or two and bring into your mind's eye an image of the ocean. If you are at the beach, just listen to the surf. Don't try to do anything with the image or sound; don't try to hold it for a long time. Just be with it, then let it fade like a spent wave receding from the shore. When you are ready, open your eyes. Your voyage into Sea Magic has begun.

THE SALT OF WISDOM

Salt has been a precious commodity since ancient times, valued for its cleansing and preservative properties and used in curing and storing food. For millennia, humans have extracted sea salt in shallow pools where it can evaporate quickly. In the past these pools were called salt gardens. Today the system is more controlled, involving greenhouses.[18]

In the days of the Roman Empire, soldiers were given an allowance of salt called *salarium*. This payment was eventually made in currency instead of salt; however the word led to our word *salary*.[19] Traditionally in Ireland, Germany, and other countries newlyweds were given a salt box with which to purify their home. The gift also symbolized the power of life.[20]

Like the ocean, salt has been revered for its mysterious qualities. *Sal sapientia* is Latin for "salt of wisdom." Salt became symbolic of wisdom, insight, and understanding.[21] The prophet Elisha noted in Second Kings (2:19–22), "What is salt, except heavenly wisdom."[22] Salt has been used as a sacrament in baptism to cleanse and sanctify.

Among medieval alchemists, the salt of wisdom, *alembroth*, was also known as philosopher's salt and was considered to have mystical properties when combined with sulfur. This substance was believed to be a step in the transmutation of base metals into gold and "whoever knows the salt, knows the secret of the ancient sages."[23] Taking the esoteric meaning of alchemy—transmutation—we have the ability to transform from a lower ego-based self to a higher soulful self. This is the basis of many meditative and spiritual practices.

---

18 Harry Wilk, *The Magic of Minerals*, 58.

19 Oskar Seyffert, *A Dictionary of Classical Antiquities, Mythology, Religion, Literature and Art*, 554.

20 Frank MacEowen, *The Mist-Filled Path*, 41.

21 C. G. Jung, *Mysterium Coniunctionis*, 242.

22 Guy Carleton Lee, *The World's Orators*, 317.

23 M. F. M. Van den Berk, *The Magic Flute: Die Zauberflöte, An Alchemical Allegory*, 144.

According to Carl Jung, salt is a symbol for the self [24] as well as the human soul and "spark of *anima mundi*" (soul of the world).[25] He also noted that the two "outstanding properties of salt are bitterness and wisdom." Tears are bitter, "but wisdom is the comforter in all psychic suffering."[26] Salt, wisdom, and comfort are all attributes of Mother Ocean—provider and teacher.

PRACTICE: SEA CENTERING

If you already use a grounding and centering technique, the sea centering meditation will feel familiar to you. The difference is that we use the ocean rather than the earth as our focal point for energy, establishing a connection with the sea on a deep inner level. Sea centering helps us find and pick up the threads of an ancient dialogue between humans and the sacred world.

In this practice, we will commune with the sea and move ocean energy in a circuit through the body from the sacrum to the crown of the head. To imagine this circuit, think of our body's three basic rhythms: the circulatory system, the breath, and the movement of cerebral spinal fluid. It's easy to think of the circulatory system with its seawater-like salty blood as representing the flowing tides of our bodies, and the breath creating the wind waves that come and go upon the face of the ocean. The cranial-sacral system with its cerebral spinal fluid represents the currents of our deep inner ocean. Because its pulse is much slower, it is a perfect focus for centering energy.

To tune in to these rhythms, we will begin this practice by using all our senses to establish a connection with the sea—using several items to help us. (These items are important at first while learning this technique, but with time, they will become less so, and you will be able to do a sea centering anywhere and anytime you need it.)

---

24 Jung, *Mysterium Coniunctionis*, 245.

25 Ibid., 241.

26 Ibid., 246.

For starters, gather the following, one for each of the five senses:

- Touch—Use a seashell or dish of sand from a beach.

- Taste—Dissolve a pinch of sea salt in a small glass of warm spring-water. (Again, avoid tap water.)

- Sound—Choose from the various seascape sound recordings on the markets. Some of these are accompanied by piano or other instruments, but for purposes of sea centering, use one with only natural sounds. Or find an inexpensive machine that provides a variety of sounds, including ocean waves.

- Scent—Finding the right odor can be tricky. After all, what does the sea smell like? (Sunblock may be part of the beachgoing experience, but it's not what you want here.) If you enjoy the smell of fresh seaweed, look for it at a local health food store. Or perhaps a particular candle captures the fragrance. Look for sea-evoking colors, too, ranging from dark blue (deep ocean) to light green (think tropical) to white (seafoam).

- Sight—Use any picture of the sea or shore that resonates with you. A photograph of a beach you have visited can be especially potent because it holds your complete experience.

Choose a room where you will have quiet privacy: a room where you regularly meditate or pray is ideal. When you are ready to begin, assemble your items there and start the music or sound machine so you can listen to the sea as you prepare. The sound will also help focus your intention and aid in the transition away from mundane consciousness. You may wish to darken the room slightly. Place the picture where you can see it clearly from a comfortable seated position. Place your candle or scent source nearby where its fragrance will reach you and its glow will add to the meditative atmosphere. Have your seashell or sand and small glass of seawater within arm's reach.

Once your space is prepared, settle comfortably in front of the items and close your eyes. Take a couple of long, slow breaths, letting your exhale last as long as your inhale, if this is comfortable for you. Scan your body for any tension and then invite those muscles to release and relax. The present moment is the only thing you need to be aware of; yesterday is over and tomorrow does not yet exist. Anything important will return to your mind when you have finished the meditation, and if it doesn't, then it wasn't truly important.

During the meditation, when other thoughts intrude, acknowledge them and then set them aside. Remind yourself that if it is important it will come back to you later. Pushing thoughts away, ignoring them, or trying to blockade them may provide more of a distraction than the thoughts themselves. If you find that your thoughts have strayed, don't be annoyed with yourself. Be glad that part of your mind realized the distraction; simply accept it and return to where you were. Despite interruptions from our chattering monkey brains, returning to the point of focus will deepen the meditation, allowing us to peel back each fine onionskin layer toward the inner self.

When you feel relaxed, shift your attention to the sea sound until it is the only thing in your awareness. When this occurs, allow your eyes to open and with a soft gaze, shift your attention to the picture, without losing awareness of the sound.

Take time for sight and sound to meld. Allow your mind to experience the sound as though it is emanating from the picture. If you are using candles, allow the flickering light to be perceived as wave motion; let yourself believe that you are watching a moving sea. When this happens, let your experience widen to take in the scents. Widen the experience again by picking up the seashell or resting one of your hands in the sand. When these become part of the experience, dip a finger in the saltwater and place a drop on your tongue.

Maintain awareness of all your senses, then close your eyes and become aware of the subsurface current of your internal ocean—the cerebral spinal fluid at your core. Feel the gentle motion of the waves here as you integrate it with the sensations from your other senses. Feel the pull of your internal ocean. The great sea is present in your sacrum—the base of the spinal column. This sacred bone represents the depths of your current. It is the undersea mountain that attaches you to this planet and the quiet, deep trench of true self. The darkness of these depths incubates and yields rich creativity which, when allowed, will rise with your current in a circuit from sacrum to crown.

From the sacrum, the primal current flows up through the core of the body, through the layers of self. At first it travels along a path that parallels the energy channel called Kurma nadi. Kurma nadi begins between the first chakra (at the perineum) and the second chakra (about two inches below the belly button) and ends at the throat chakra. According to Pandit Rajmani Tigunait, this energy channel "regulates the stability of body and mind."[27] That's a perfect combination for sea centering. It is also appropriate because of its name: Kurma was the second incarnation of the Hindu god Vishnu who, in the form of a great sea turtle, carried the world on his back. Kurma also carried on his back Shesha naga, the cosmic snake representing the great mother goddess, symbolizing a balance of male and female energies.

Now our inner current passes the heart center, where compassion adds warmth and spirit. As the current rises, the energy passes the throat chakra. The sea's voice can laugh, sing, or roar, and likewise, we can express our thoughts and feelings in many ways.

But now our inner sea moves beyond the Kurma nadi and circles the brain, just as the ancient mythological oceans encircled the human realm. The sea—and water in general—is associated with wisdom. Warmed on the sunny mounts exposed to the heavens, our sea soaks in a beauty and grace that is both personal and universal, private and public, new with each breath and yet timeless. This ancient tide is always changing, yet ever-constant. Let your current stay suspended here, almost to stillness, nourished with wisdom and compassion. Then let it sink back to the depths of the sacred mountain to renew the inner self. This current's energy provides the buoyancy that will let new and different aspects of self rise to the surface on the next wave. Minute by minute we change and evolve, like a beach tended by Mother Ocean.

When you have followed a complete circuit of energy—sacrum to crown and back—allow your mind and senses to let go of the experience. Reconnect with your breath and the room in which you sit. Give your-

---

27 Pandit Rajmani Tigunait, *Inner Quest*, 146–147.

self time to make the transition back to your everyday world. Pick up the threads of your life, but know and feel the journey you have taken. Feel the new depths you have found and the connection you have forged. Know that you can return here to find your center and reestablish your unique place in this world.

Repeat this exercise a few times or more until you can create the experience without using the "tools" for the senses: the picture, the sand, and so on. Once you can go through the complete process—when you can see, smell, hear, touch, and taste the sea and move through the entire experience—you have gained the ability to do a sea centering. It may take a little practice, and you may want to return to using your tools from time to time to keep your senses in tune. Sometimes only one or two tools may be enough to reestablish this centering to its full extent. Trust your intuition to find what works best for you.

A sea centering has effects similar to grounding and centering, the difference being that the solid grounded feeling is accompanied by a sense of fluidity. While this may sound contradictory, once you have experienced this sensation, you will remember it deep in your body.

You may want to journal your experiences with sea centering. Over time, this written record becomes a valuable repository of information about yourself, and can offer a way to discover and unite threads that may otherwise remain obscure.

THE OCEANIC REALM OF EMOTION

The emotional realm is related to the element of water, and working with Sea Magic brings us deeply into this area of our psyches. As it connects us with our inner ocean, the sea centering practice gives us the stability to deal with and explore our emotions.

If left to stagnate, emotions, just like water, can turn toxic. You may find that as you do the sea centering practice, a cleansing process will begin. As you follow that movement of energy from the depths of your inner ocean, old emotions may be stirred and even brought to the surface of your conscious mind. Become aware of this if it occurs; allow things to surface, and then, more importantly, let them go.

Frequently, when the emotional depths are disturbed, what rises is not any particular feeling; nothing is clearly identifiable. It is not important to figure out exactly where it came from. What is important is to allow yourself to release whatever comes up. Your emotional self is getting rid of something it doesn't need. Allow the energy of the Kurma nadi to release it. Since this energy channel ends at the throat, you can give expression to this release literally or symbolically. Verbally, you can acknowledge it by saying: "I don't know what this feeling is, but I release it from my being and I cleanse my spirit."

Alternatively, you could cry, shout, or sing, or use the ocean breath (see the following description) to aid in releasing these emotions. When you feel that something has been released, visualize your inner ocean washing clean the space that once held those emotions. Feel refreshed. If things come up that are challenging, give yourself time to heal. Know that by exploring your inner world you are showing love and compassion for yourself, which is not a selfish act.

If you do not experience any sort of emotional release, that's okay. You may not need to get rid of anything. Maybe you are ready to move deeper. Working with the sea centering provides the opportunity to dive deep into our inner worlds—not only of emotion, but also of imagination and creativity. Dr. Wayne Dyer has said that "imagination is the movement of the universal mind within you."[28]

The inner child is a part of who we are as adults. Just as we are able to relax and play at the beach, so too should we be able to do this at other times and places. The ocean, inner or global, helps us to play, which is essentially about experiencing joy.

Our culture teaches us that we have to constantly do things ("Just do it!"), to take charge and get things done. However, there are times in life when we simply need to float, to go with the ebb and flow of things. There are certain times and situations when, from deep down, our intuitive voices tell us to let things be. When this occurs, try to float. It doesn't mean that you relinquish all control or you don't care. It means that you have

---

28 Wayne Dyer, *The Power of Intention*, 38.

faith in yourself as well as divine universal guidance. You will know when to begin swimming toward shore.

In general, the element water is connected with nourishment, rest, and regeneration. As we work with the sea centering practice, following our ebb and flow, we eventually find that we have within us the ability to nourish our souls and perhaps go through a process of transformation. This sea change is the merging of our inner and outer selves; we each become the person we were truly meant to be. Finding that we can love ourselves allows us to step into a wider world and live more fully in the vast ocean of life.

In addition to love, one of the most uplifting emotions is gratitude. We know that our existence is part of divine universal energy, and it is a tremendous gift. When we see our lives as gifts, we truly cherish who we are and live close to the magic and mystery of the natural world.

PRACTICE: OCEAN BREATH

The breath is like the tide coming in and going out again in regular rhythm, as John O'Donohue noted.[29] At one time the breath was thought to be the route by which the soul entered the body, making it the "sister of spirit."[30] Inspiration is the act of taking air into the body, absorbing the life-force energy that each living cell needs. The word *inspiration* also means "divine influence." Dr. Wayne Dyer said that "the word *inspiration* means 'in-spirit,'" and that spirit is "working through you."[31]

A breathing technique and meditative tool called "ocean breath" is known by most yoga practitioners by its Sanskrit name *ujjayi*. Quite simply, we make an ocean sound on the "inspiration" and the exhalation of each breath.

Begin by pretending to fog a mirror with your breath: hold your hand a couple of inches from your mouth and make a gentle *hhhaaa* sound from the back of your throat as you exhale against your hand. Inhale in the same

---

29 John O'Donohue, *Anam Cara*, 163–164.

30 Ibid., 69.

31 Dyer, *Power of Intention*, 102, 5.

way, making the same sound. The inhalation may be a little more challenging at first. After you have done this a few times, close your mouth and continue to make the sound as you breathe in and out. The sound should be subtle; no one but you needs to hear it. Close your eyes and visualize the surf gently breaking upon the shore and withdrawing.

This breathing technique is a good tool to use to begin a sea centering or any type of meditation. It can also be useful at bedtime to quiet the mind as you prepare for sleep. You may also want to try using your sea-sounds machine or recording at bedtime to set your intention to dream of the sea, or to prepare for a subconscious sea centering while you sleep. You may want to journal about any dreams or thoughts and sensations afterward.

Using sea centering and ocean breath is especially important if you cannot often visit the ocean. It may take a little more work to visualize, but your intention is enough for you to draw on the magic of the sea.

Now that we have crossed the beach, stepped over the Sea Magic threshold, and waded in, we can chart our course into Mother Ocean's wondrous realm.

JOURNAL QUESTIONS

1. What does the word *magic* mean to you?

2. What does water mean to you—in general, and ocean water specifically?

3. What have you felt while watching the ocean? If you have never been to the ocean, what do you imagine you would feel?

4. What sensations did you experience with the sea centering practice? Was it similar to feeling grounded or what there a clear difference for you?

II

MYTHS, DEITIES, AND SAINTS

...*A*nd some upon day's shores are cast,
And some in darkness lost
In waves beyond the world, where float
Somewhere the islands of the blest.

KATHLEEN RAINE,
Nocturn

WHILE WE HAVE A CERTAIN at-homeness *with* the sea and to a certain extent feel that we belong there, we are not completely at home *on* the sea because we lack the ability to control it. The ocean is unstable and ever-changing, keeping us at our edge. It is a mesmerizing netherworld, a neverland that floats between the worlds. It is soothing and yet dangerous. Because it is a realm of deep mystery, people through the ages have turned to the ocean to seek answers to life's conundrums, to seek patterns in the inexplicable. After all, if gods and angels could live in the sky, they could live in the sea. People of antiquity believed that there was "a controlling or animating spirit of the ocean."[1]

The word *myth* originally meant "a sacred story, appertaining to the divine," according to Jean Markale.[2] Myths contained powerful archetypes and conveyed meaningful lessons; they still do. In ancient times they also served to bring order to the world, to make it more understandable. Arthur Cotterell and Rachel Storm noted that "creation myths have evolved in every culture, often with striking similarities such as the limitless ocean from which the universe arises."[3] The primordial and chaotic mothers of water were depicted as the deities Tamtu, Tiamat, and Tiawath by the Babylonians; Tohu and Tchom by the Hebrews; and Nun and Nu by the Egyptians.[4] In Nordic myth, not only did the world

---

1 Lewis Spence, *The Minor Traditions of British Mythology*, 56.

2 Jean Markale, *The Celts*, 14.

3 Arthur Cotterell and Rachel Storm, *The Ultimate Encyclopedia of Mythology*, 9.

4 Egerton Sykes, *Everyman's Dictionary of Non-Classical Mythology*, 66.

begin as a vast chaotic ocean, but it was believed that at the end of days the land would sink back into the sea.[5]

According to some versions of the Babylonian myth, in the beginning only an abyss of water existed, an abyss that was split by the god Belus to create heaven and earth.[6] In the Mesopotamian take on it, the cosmos came into existence when two primordial oceans merged: Apsu, the freshwater ocean, and Tiamat, the saltwater.[7] Waves created by Tiamat gave rise to the first divine couples from whom all other gods descended.[8] According to Carl Jung, the sea was thought of as a "matrix of all creatures. The *prima materia* is often called *aqua pontica*."[9] In other words, the primal material, the base of all physical matter, is seawater.

Some creation myths combined the concept of the cosmic egg and the ocean. In Finnish myth, Luonnotar, the goddess of creation and daughter of nature, was alone in the primordial ocean until an eagle made a nest on her knee. She accidentally dropped the nest into the sea, where the broken eggs became the earth and sky. On the other side of the world in Borneo, the spirits Ara and Irik floated in the boundless ocean in which they discovered two eggs that became the sky and the land.[10]

Not only do myths portray the primeval ocean as the source of the world and life, they also depict the sea's power to wipe the slate clean and start over. In addition to the Bible, stories from India, the Mediterranean region, and the Americas tell of a great deluge in which the sea covered the earth as a form of cleansing. Perhaps for this reason sailors have traditionally regarded seafaring as "a kind of spiritual purity."[11]

Many early villages and cities were built on the seacoast for the simple reason that the ocean provided abundant food. As a result, it was natural to give thanks for the provider who nourished and sustained the life of

---

5 D. J. Conway, *Norse Magic*, 140.

6 Sykes, *Everyman's Dictionary*, 27.

7 Cotterell and Storm, *Ultimate Encyclopedia of Mythology*, 264.

8 Sykes, *Everyman's Dictionary*, 210.

9 Jung, *Mysterium Coniunctionis*, 193.

10 Cotterell and Storm, *Ultimate Encyclopedia of Mythology*, 209, 426.

11 Horace Beck, *Folklore and the Sea*, 300.

the village. The people of Peru worshipped Mama Choca, Mother Sea; the Inuit of Alaska gave thanks to Nerrivik; the Yoruba of Africa honored Yemanja. Some Greek sailors invoked the help of Panope and Thetis— two of the Nereids—while others venerated Glaucus, a son of Poseidon. In China, sailors kept shrines to the sea goddess Tien-How aboard their boats.[12]

A ritual to placate sea spirits before embarking on a voyage was customary for the Romans, Vikings, and others. Breaking a bottle of champagne on the bow of a new ship at its naming is a modern echo of this ancient tribute to sea spirits.[13]

Like the sea itself, sea spirits and deities were portrayed as beautiful and mysterious as well as treacherous. And, like the ever-changing sea and its shoreline, many of these deities were by nature shape-shifters: they could come ashore and assume the shape of land dwellers.

More than anything, the ocean has been venerated for its sheer power; it cannot be conquered by humankind. Deities, of course, take on super-human tasks: The Hindu god Kurma, mentioned earlier, lifted Mount Mandara out of the churning waters to preserve the world; the Roman god Neptune could trigger earthquakes; the Norse god Njord could calm winter storms.

Dynamic and restless, the waves were considered animate beings by some peoples. When heavy seas broke upon the shores of Ireland, they were said to be "the white horses of Manannan."[14] The god Phorcus represented the white seafoam and was the keeper of sea monsters. The Greeks frequently personified the waves as wild bulls as well as sheep. Breakers have been referred to as "Neptune's white herds," and in French they are called *moutons*, meaning "sheep."[15]

In addition to the gift of food, the sea provides precious salt with which to flavor and preserve it. One Nordic myth explains the salt in seawater: King Mysing had a special mill aboard his ship and took captives

---

12 Bassett, *Legends and Superstitions*, 61–63, 74.

13 Anna Franklin, *Illustrated Encyclopedia of Fairies*, 227.

14 M. Oldfield Howey, *The Horse in Magic and Myth*, 143.

15 Bassett, *Legends and Superstitions*, 23–24.

as slaves to grind salt. When the ship sank under the weight of its cargo, water rushed through the hole in the millstone, creating a whirlpool.[16] This stirred the salt and spread it throughout the ocean.

As cultures developed, so too did their myths and pantheons. It is no surprise that the classical civilization of Greece—which rose on a peninsula in the Mediterranean—had the largest number of sea gods, goddesses, and minor oceanic deities. The ancient Greeks called the Mediterranean *Thalassa* and believed that it divided the earth east and west, beyond which the giant ocean *Okeanes* surrounded all the land. The Romans called the Mediterranean *Mare Nostrum*, "Our Sea," and the unexplored Atlantic *Mare Tenebrosum*, "Sea of Darkness."[17]

Greek mythology tells us about two dynasties of sea deities. The earliest began with Oceanus and Tethys, the second with Pontus and Gaia. These two great families were joined with the marriage of Doris (daughter of Oceanus and Tethys) and Nereus (son of Pontus and Gaia) in a union that produced fifty sea nymphs known as the Nereids. (Accounts differ as to the actual number of Nereids.) These deities' powers extended beyond the sea, too: Poseidon and Amphitrite also controlled the winds, as did Triton, their son, to a lesser extent. Interestingly, ocean deities also brought forth the arts and sciences. Proteus and Nereus gave humans wisdom. Nereus also had prophetic powers. Although Apollo is not a sea deity, he was venerated by sailors as Apollo Delphinus: disguised as a dolphin, he was said to have led an endangered ship to safety.[18]

For a time, early Christian sailors from Norway continued to call on Thor when in danger at sea.[19] However, as Christianity spread, Jesus, Mary, and a number of saints took the place of the old gods and goddesses. In addition to Stella Maris, the Virgin Mary was also called "Our Lady of the Waves" and became the patroness of many seaside chapels. She was believed to have saved many ships from wreck by guiding them to port or calming a storm. Fishermen considered St. Anthony one of the most powerful saints

---

16 Viktor Rydberg, *Teutonic Myth*, 387.

17 Bassett, *Legends and Superstitions*, 14.

18 Ibid., 63.

19 Ibid., 7.

for protection, and many Portuguese ships carried a statue of him onboard. St. Nicholas figured high in accounts of pilgrims traveling by water to and from the Holy Land. In addition to quelling storms caused by the devil's tricks, he was said to have "restored a sailor to life."[20] As the fisher apostle, St. Peter was also called upon for deliverance from peril, and the dragon-slayer St. George was invoked for protection against sea monsters.

HIDDEN LANDS

As an element of transformation, water is associated with darkness, mystery and death as well as regeneration, beauty, and peace. Many legends speak of a land of ancestral spirits that lies beneath the waves or at the edge of the known world. Not all of these places were watery versions of hell; some were beautiful and pleasant. Departing souls would pass through these lands on their way to heaven, rebirth, or an eternity in paradise. Some stories encompass both extremes. Sailors believed that if they died at sea they would end up in one of two places, depending on their behavior in life: either Davy Jones' Locker—a euphemism for the devil and hell—or Fiddler's Green, a paradise under the sea.[21]

This belief in some kind of blessed isle beneath the waves or just beyond the horizon was shared by ancient Egyptians, Sumerians, Greeks,[22] Celts, and others. The Celtic *imram* stories tell of magical sea voyages in which wanderers are guided through otherworldly adventures. In some, the islands visited represent states of consciousness, gates of power, or stages of initiation.[23] St. Brendan made a legendary voyage seeking the Promised Land of the Saints and claimed to have glimpsed the Blessed Isle.[24]

Journeys to these hidden places represent exploration, transformation (rebirth), and growth. Venturing into deep water—a symbol for the

---

20 Ibid., 76, 78.

21 Horace Beck, *Folklore and the Sea*, 281.

22 Andrew Collings, *Gateway to Atlantis*, 83.

23 Frank MacEowen, *The Mist-Filled Path*, 71.

24 Shirley Toulson, *The Celtic Year*, 148.

inner self as well as emotion—can be frightening. Like water, these mystical and symbolic journeys are spiritually cleansing.

These islands and other worlds were known by many names. The British Isles had Avalon (Emain Ablach, or Isle of Apples).[25] Ireland had the Land of Promise (Tír Tairngiri)[26] ruled by sea god Manannan, the Land of the Ever Young (Tír na nÓg),[27] and the Isle of Beauty (Hy Braesal).[28] The Greeks and Romans had the Elysian Fields, their version of a joyous Otherworld flowing with good food and drink.[29]

Some myths held that these hidden worlds were occasionally visible on the horizon. When one gazes west off the Irish coast, the Aran Islands may seem to float there in the mist—a mystical place, in the view of earlier peoples. When I was on pilgrimage on Inis Mór (Isle of the Sea), I sat on the raised platform of rock near the cliff's edge at Dún Aengus and gazed out to sea, pondering these stories and wishing that I might catch a glimpse of those magical places. As I watched waves form and dissipate beyond the misty horizon where the ninth wave beckons, I thought of the words of John O'Donohue:"The visible is only one little edge of things. The visible is only the shoreline of the magnificent ocean of the invisible."[30]

WORKING WITH SEA DEITIES AND SAINTS

Working with a sea god or goddess provides a way to connect with the sea's energy; it is not a form of worship. Ancient peoples created pantheons to put a human face on the world's mysteries, searching for logic in the inexplicable powers of nature. Similarly, working with a deity can link us with this vast energy, making it more tangible. Putting a human face on it helps us personalize our experiences.

---

25 Markale, *Celts*, 46.

26 Franklin, *Illustrated Encyclopedia of Fairies*, 250.

27 James MacKillop, *Oxford Dictionary of Celtic Mythology*, 406.

28 Ibid., 267.

29 Ibid., 359.

30 John O'Donohue, *Eternal Echoes*, 126.

Working with sea deities and saints begins by learning about them: this section contains a multicultural pantheon for you to choose from. If you feel attracted to a certain deity you may want to do further research to learn more. Alternatively, working with the energy of a particular saint or the Virgin Mary may feel more appropriate. Explore to find what works best for you.

If you are not sure where to begin, start with your own background. If you are in the melting pot of America, consider where your family originated. Perhaps it was a country or region of seafaring people with oceanic myths. Or perhaps you are attracted to a particular pantheon of sea deities because their stories resonate with you. On the other hand, if you have studied mythology or art history, the fantastic imagery of Greece's classical gods and goddesses may be alive in your heart. These various inroads provide a starting point for finding the ones that suit you. You may also find that you prefer to work with the energies of various deities or saints at various times. There are no limitations; allow your intuition to guide you.

You may also find that any specific personification seems too narrow for something that covers most of the globe. Personally, I find that "Mother Ocean" best addresses the vastness and greatness of the watery realms, so I use this most often. That said, I have found this verse from John Milton's *Comus* very compelling for stirring Sea Magic energy. It also entices us to learn more about these ancient deities.

> In the name of great Oceanus,
> By the earth-shaking Neptune's mace
> And Tethys' grave majestic pace,
> By hoary Nereus' wrinkled look,
> And the Carpathian wizard's hook,
> By scaly Triton's winding shell,
> And old soothsaying Glaucus' spell,
> By Leucothea's lovely hands,
> And her son that rules the strands,
> By Thetis' tinsel-slippered feet,
> And the songs of Sirens sweet,
> By dead Parthenope's dear tomb,
> And fair Ligea's golden comb,
> Wherewith she sits on diamond rocks,

Sleeking her soft alluring locks.
By all the nymphs that nightly dance
Upon thy streams with wily glance,
Rise, rise, and heave thy rosy head
From thy coral-paven bed,
And bridle in thy headlong wave,
Till thou our summons answered have.[31]

As with all aspects of a spiritual or meditative practice, calling on a particular deity, group of deities, or saints is a highly personal matter. We all must follow our own heart-of-hearts and do what is most appropriate. Throughout this book, wherever I suggest calling on Mother Ocean, it is up to you to adjust that call to your personal path. Working with gods, goddesses, and saints can help bring to life certain aspects of human encounters with the ocean. But in the end, it is a tool for accessing deep and vast levels of energy. It provides a way to reach into our soul and let our spirit swim free.

A PANTHEON OF SEA DEITIES AND SAINTS

While Greek and Norse sea deities are plentiful, sea gods and goddesses can be found all over the world. This list offers an introduction and overview of the rich and varied range of deities and saints from many cultures. You may want to pursue further study of those who resonate with you.

Aegir / Aeger—Norway. The son of sea giant Fornjot and a sea god in his own right. Aegir was also the brewer for the gods, portrayed with a long, foamy beard and black helmet. The wild North Sea was sometimes called "Aegir's Brewing Kettle."[32] With his wife, Ran, he had nine daughters who were called the Vana-Mothers and personified the waves. Vikings made sacrifice to Aegir before voyages. *Associations:* MONDAY, THE MOON.

---

31 John Milton, *Comus*, 41-42.

32 Cotterell and Storm, *Ultimate Encyclopedia of Mythology*, 180.

Ahes—Brittany, France. A goddess who symbolized the sea's abundance. *Associations:* ABUNDANCE, COURAGE, FERTILITY.

Ahti / Ahto—Finland. A deity helpful to fishermen whose kingdom was in the deep abyss. Known as the Lord of the Waves,[33] he was the owner of a talisman made of magical metals. He was also known for creating whirlpools. His wife was the sea goddess Wellamo.

Akaenga—Polynesia. Master of the lower waves.

Albion—Greece. A son of Poseidon who was associated with the white-capped waves. The British Isles' poetic name *Albion* can perhaps be traced to him, possibly because the white cliffs on England's south coast resemble the whitecaps in the choppy waters of the English Channel.

Amathaounta—Greece. A sea goddess of the Aegean, also known in Palestine as Amathaon. Her worshippers, the Amathites, are mentioned in the Bible.

Amphitrite—Greece. One of the Nereids (daughters of Nereus and Doris) and wife of Poseidon. Known as the Queen of the Moaning Sea, she employed sea monsters to thrust waves onto rocky shores. Amphitrite was depicted riding in a boat of mussel shells, her wet hair in a net. Her name means "wearing away the shore."[34] *Associations:* DOLPHINS, MUSSELS, SINGING, SPINNING, WEAVING.

Angeyja—Norway. One of the Vana-Mothers who personified the waves. Daughter of Aegir and Ran.

Anne, Saint—Brittany, France, Canada, and England. Patron saint of Canadian mariners, called on when in great danger. Miracles of saving ships were attributed to her.

Anthony, Saint—Italy and Portugal. A Portuguese-born priest of Padua, Italy. He is known for preaching a sermon to the fishes. Sixteenth-century Portuguese sailors kept statues of him onboard their ships and appealed to him for favorable winds.

---

33 Bassett, *Legends and Superstitions*, 69.

34 Gertrude Jobes, *Dictionary of Mythology Folklore and Symbols*, 88.

Amphitrite

Aphrodite—Greece. A goddess of beauty and love who was "sea-foam-born."[35] Although her name comes from the word *aphros* meaning foam, she had limited power over the waves.[36] She was also called Aphrodite Marina ("of the sea"). Her designation as "All-Shining One" was a reference to her connection with the moon.[37] *Associations:* DOLPHINS, PEARLS, SCALLOP SHELLS.

Asheratian—Phoenicia. A sea goddess of creation myth who was called the Ashera of the Sea[38] and mother of the gods. She was a variant of Ashtarte. To the Semitic people she was known as Elat.

Atargatis—Syria. The queen of waters, who was hatched from an egg that fell into the sea from heaven. Atargatis was portrayed as a mermaid and her devotees were not permitted to eat fish. She was also known in Greco-Roman cultures.

---

35 Clare Gibson, *Goddess Symbols*, 38–39.

36 Bassett, *Legends and Superstitions*, 61.

37 Jules Cashford, *Moon*, 80.

38 Sykes, *Everyman's Dictionary*, 170.

Athirat—Canaan. The benevolent mother goddess known as Lady Athirat of the Sea[39] who was the wife of El and mother of storm god Baal. *Association:* SPINDLES.

Barinthus—Wales. A sea deity who was also a god of the dead. Barinthus was also the name of the boatman who ferried King Arthur's body to Avalon.

Batara Guru—Southeast Asia. Shiva, the Hindu god of creation and destruction, was known by this name in Southeast Asia. While he was primarily a sky god, in Java, Bali, and Sumatra he was also a sea god.

Benten—Japan (Shinto). A goddess of love and the sea, and a deity of good fortune and learning. She was depicted riding a dragon or serpent. *Association:* GOOD LUCK.

Brendan, Saint—Ireland. A seventh-century monk who voyaged with fourteen companions and became a patron saint of sailors. One of many legends about St. Brendan tells of sea creatures coming to the surface to hear him sing. He became known as Brendan the Navigator and was said to have reached America.

Callirrhoe—Greece. An ocean nymph, daughter of the god Oceanus.

Canente / Canens—Italy (Roman). An ocean nymph. In grief over her husband's death, Canente faded to become the singing of the waves. In some accounts she was portrayed as the wife of Neptune. She was also known as Salacia.

Ceto—Greece. One of the Nereids (daughters of Nereus and Doris). She personified the "hidden pearls of the sea."[40]

Chalchiuhtlicue—Mexico (Aztec). A sea goddess venerated by seafaring fishermen. Her aspects included Acuecueyotl, who created the ocean swells; Alauh, the mist and spray; Apoconalloti, seafoam; Atlacamani, sea storms; Xixiquiphilihui, the rising and falling of waves. *Associations:* TURQUOISE, JADEITE.

---

39 Clare Gibson, *Goddess Symbols*, 23.

40 Jobes, *Dictionary of Mythology*, 306.

Cliodhna—Ireland. A goddess of beauty who was lured back to the Otherworld by a giant wave sent by Manannan mac Lir. The third wave in a series of three is called Cliodhna's wave.[41]

Clytie—Greece. A sea nymph and daughter of Oceanus. Clytie was in love with the sun god Helios.

Columba, Saint—Scotland. A sixth-century monk who became a popular marine saint of the British Isles. In addition to prophetic knowledge, he was said to have the power to command the ocean and raise a wind.

Cyric, Saint—Wales. A patron saint called on by Welsh mariners and people on pilgrimage. He was called Ruler of the Waves.[42]

Dagon—Philistia. A sea god who was also the Philistines' chief deity. He was depicted with a human face and hands but a fish tail instead of legs. He was known as Oannes in other cultures. As Dagon, he is mentioned in the Bible in the books of Samuel, Judges, Joshua, and Chronicles. *Associations:* ABUNDANCE, FERTILITY, FRUITFULNESS, ZODIAC SIGN OF CAPRICORN.

Danwantaree—India (Hindu). A god who rose from the sea to bring gifts to the human race.

Derceto—Babylon. A sea goddess who, like Aphrodite, sprang from the sea. On ancient coins she was depicted with the moon above her head and a mermaid at her feet.[43] Derceto herself was occasionally portrayed with the body of a fish. She may have been the same or sometimes confused with the Syrian Atargatis.

Domnu—Ireland. Fomorian goddess of the deep sea and symbol of wisdom.

Doris—Greece. Sea goddess, daughter of Oceanus and Tethys and wife of Nereus. Her sea-nymph daughters were the Nereids, who personified the countless waves.

---

41 Cotterell and Storm, *Ultimate Encyclopedia of Mythology*, 115.

42 Bassett, *Legends and Superstitions*, 82.

43 Ibid., 57.

Drebkuls—Latvia. A sea deity who could make the earth shake.

Dsovean—Armenia. A sea god of storms. Dsovinar was his female counterpart.

Dylan—Wales. The son of Arianrhod who leapt away from her at birth and into the sea to become known as the Son of the Waves. The incoming tide echoes the lament of the waves at his death.

Endil—Scandinavia. The sea was sometimes referred to as Endil's meadow. Sailors were called the sons of Endil.[44]

Eurybia—Greece. A sea nymph and one of the Nereids, daughters of Nereus and Doris. *Associations:* DOLPHINS, SINGING, SPINNING, WEAVING.

Eyrgjafa—Norway. One of the Vana-Mothers who personified the waves. Daughter of Aegir and Ran. Her name means "sand strewer,"[45] and she was believed responsible for creating sand bars.

Fomorians—Ireland and Scotland. A sea race of early gods who represented darkness. Their name means "sea giant," and their fortress was near Tory Island. They ventured ashore to demand tribute and do battle. They were also known as the Fomhairs in Scotland.

Fornjot—Norway. An ocean giant whose kingdom, Vanaheim, was located below the western sea. He was also a storm god.

Gaiar—Ireland and Isle of Man. A deity of the sea and the underworld; son of Manannan.

Galatea—Greece. A sea nymph and one of the Nereids (daughters of Nereus and Doris). To avoid the pursuing Cyclops, she turned her lover, a shepherd named Acis, into a river so they could unite as water. She is described riding in a chariot pulled by dolphins. *Associations:* DOLPHINS, SINGING, SPINNING, WEAVING.

---

44 Grenville Pigott and Adam Gottlob Oehlenschläger, *A Manual of Scandinavian Mythology*, 309.

45 Henry Adams Bellows (translator), *The Poetic Edda*, 229.

George, Saint—England. In addition to slaying the dragon, Saint George was believed to have power over its marine counterpart, the sea serpent. Sardinian fishermen appealed to him for help.

Glaucus—Greece. A son of Poseidon who was venerated by fishermen.

Guabonito—Carribean (Taino Indian). A woman who rose from the sea and taught people to use amulets.

Haya-Akitsu—Japan. A female deity who could calm raging seas. She made her home at the "meeting places of the tides . . . and sea paths."[46]

Hina-Ika—Polynesia. The sea goddess who created fishing nets from the silver rays of her hair. Also known as Lady of the Fish, she is a form of Hine, the moon goddess.[47]

Hine-Te-Ngaru-Moana—New Zealand (Maori). A mermaid form of Hine, the moon goddess who controlled the tides. She was known as Lady of the Waves.[48]

Ishara—Mesopotamia. A sea goddess known along the Phoenician coast in the form of a scorpion. She accompanied Inanna/Ishtar when depicted as a goddess of death. She was known as Ishara of the Sea.[49]

Ixchel—Central America (Mayan). Although a moon goddess, she was also known as Lady Sea because the moon appeared to rise from the sea. Her shrine was on Isla Mujeres.

Jaladhija—India (Hindu). Vishnu's consort Lakshmi was also known by this name, which means "ocean born." Like Aphrodite, Jaladhija arose from the sea fully formed. She was also known as Ksirabdhitanaya, "daughter of the ocean."

---

46 William Aston, *A History of Japanese Literature*, 12.

47 Cashford, *Moon*, 79.

48 Ibid.

49 Theophilus Pinches, *The Religion of Babylonia and Assyria*, 54.

The Mayan moon goddess Ixchel was also known as Lady Sea.

James the Greater, Saint—Palestine and Spain. An apostle and patron saint of Spanish sailors. He was said to have sailed to Spain from Palestine in a marble ship. A fisherman by trade, James was summoned from Galilee by Jesus to become a fisher of men. The shrine to him at Compostela became the site of pilgrimage.

Komokoa—Pacific Northwest. A Native American sea deity who protected seals and took in the souls of those who drowned.

Kurma—India (Hindu). The second incarnation of Vishnu, in the form of a sea turtle that lifted Mount Mandara out of the waters on his back during the churning of the oceans. This act represented the manifestation and preservation of the world. Indeed, preserving the world is Vishnu's eternal task.

Leucothea—Greece. A deity who was originally a mortal named Ino. Through a sea change instituted by the gods, she became a sea goddess when she fled her husband and threw herself with her son into the ocean. She used her power to save shipwrecked sailors, among them Odysseus in

Homer's *Odyssey*. Her name means "white goddess."[50] Her son, Palaemon, was better known as the Roman Portumnus.

Lir / Llyr—Ireland and Wales. A sea god who is most famous for his son Manannan. In Irish lore, Lir's four other children were turned into swans by their jealous stepmother and doomed to spend nine hundred years in the icy northern seas. The Welsh Llyr's children included Branwen and Bendigeidfran/Bran the Blessed.

Mama Cocha—Peru. An ocean mother goddess worshipped by fishermen as a nurturer and provider. The Chinchas people called her Mother Sea[51] and believed that everything, including themselves, came from her. *Associations:* ABUNDANCE, NURTURING, PROTECTION.

Manannan mac Lir—Ireland. A sea god and healer who ruled Tír-na-nOg, the Otherworld, believed to be located off the west coast of Ireland. His wife was Fand, but he had many lovers (and children), both mortal and divine. He possessed a ship, called Wave Sweeper, that could sail itself. Manannan aided some sea voyagers and hindered others.

Manawydan mac Llyr—Wales. The Welsh counterpart of Manannan mac Lir, but a lesser sea god. His wife was Rhiannon.

Mark the Evangelist, Saint—Italy and Palestine. The patron saint of Venetian fishermen, who saluted his statue when departing on a voyage. It was said that the seas became calm when his body was being returned from Egypt.

Michael the Archangel—The archangel said to possess power over the sea and wind, also called the Neptune of the Gael.[52] The most famous places dedicated to him are the two Mounts St. Michael in Brittany, France and Cornwall, England. He is patron saint of ships, sailors, and maritime lands.

---

50 Jobes, *Dictionary of Mythology*, 988.

51 Alexander Chamberlain, *The Child and Childhood in Folk Thought*, 89.

52 Alexander Carmichael (translator), *Carmina Gadelica*, 200.

Mimir—Norway. The god of the primeval sea who embodied the power of the four elements. The open sea was sometimes referred to as Mimir's Well. Drinking from this magical water, believed to be found at the root of Yggdrasil (world tree), imparted great wisdom. *Associations:* MEAD, ORACULAR KNOWLEDGE, THE RUNES MANNAZ (MEMORY), ANSUZ (INSPIRATION), KENAZ (KNOWLEDGE).

Mommu—Babylon. The dark, primeval ocean from whose womb Lakhmu, the sea monster, emerged. In some legends she served Tiamat; in others, Mommu was another name for Tiamat.

Morskoi Tzar—Russia. Ruler of the kingdom below the waves, and described as a Slavonic Neptune.[53] He lived in the depths of the sea. His daughters wore feathered dresses to go ashore and were known as Swan Maidens.

Naètè—Africa (Fon of Benin). She became a sea goddess when her mother, the great goddess Mawu, told her to "go and inhabit the sea, and command the waters."[54]

Nanshe—Babylon and Sumer. Goddess of the sea and fish. Nanshe's worship was centered in the city of Nina in southern Babylon, and in the earlier Sumerian city of Lagash. She served as an arbiter of judgment and was celebrated on January first. *Associations:* DREAMS, JUSTICE, PREMONITIONS.

Neptune—Italy (Roman). Counterpart to the Greek Poseidon. Neptune's worship centered in the cities of Calabria, Corinth, and Taenarus, where he was celebrated on July 23 during the dry season. Believed to both protect the earth and cause earthquakes, Neptune was depicted riding in a large shell pulled by sea horses and whales. His wife was the goddess of saltwater, Salacia. The trident was his symbol of power. The first formal shell-collecting organization, dating from 1720, called itself the Lovers of Neptune's Cabinet. *Associations:* DOLPHINS, SEA HORSES, WHALES.

---

53 W. R. S. Ralston, *Songs of the Russian People*, 148.

54 Melville and Frances Herskovits, *Dahomean Narrative*, 125.

Nereids—Greece. The sea nymph daughters of Nereus and Doris, who personify the ocean's countless waves. They lived at the bottom of the sea in their father's palace where they sat upon thrones of gold. *Associations:* DOLPHINS, SINGING, SPINNING, WEAVING.

Nereus—Greece. Son of Pontus (the high seas) and Gaia (earth). He represented the elemental forces and personified calm seas. Considered benevolent, he was sometimes referred to as the Old Man of the Sea.[55] With his wife, Doris, he fathered the Nereids, sea nymphs. He was depicted with a white beard and seaweed for hair, and the trident was his symbol of power, as it was for Neptune. *Associations:* BALANCE AND HARMONY, TRANSFORMATION.

Nerrivik—Alaska (Inuit). A sea goddess and sea spirit believed to be the source of all life. She ruled over sea creatures and all who passed beyond the veil of life, including humans. When food was scarce she was called upon to release seals and other animals to be hunted. She was called Food Dish,[56] referring to her aspect of provider and nourisher. She is also known as Arnarkusaga or Arnakuagsak in Greenland and Sedna in Canada.

Niamh—Ireland. The daughter of Manannan who "personified the radiant beauty of the sea."[57] She lived in Tíi-na-nOg with her husband Oisin and was sometimes called "Niamh of the Golden Hair."[58]

Nicholas, Saint—Italy. The sailor's guardian who was said to have brought a sailor back to life while on voyage to the Holy Land. He was also said to have saved ships from sinking in storms, most notably one of King Richard's in 1190. Many chapels were dedicated to him and a statue of him near Liverpool, England, was a popular place for sailors to leave votive offerings.

---

55 Pierre Grimal, *The Dictionary of Classical Mythology*, 308.

56 Hartley Alexander, *North American Mythology*, 6.

57 Jobes, *Dictionary of Mythology*, 1167.

58 Cotterell and Storm, *Ultimate Encyclopedia of Mythology*, 148.

Nerrivik

Njord—Norway. The oldest of the Vanir gods, whose name means "strength."[59] He was a god of ships, sailors, beaches, and seacoasts who helped sailors with good winds and good fortune in hunting. He calmed winter storms and represented the mild coastal sea. He had beautiful feet—a footprint is his symbol representing a sandy beach. He is depicted wearing a crown of seashells. *Associations:* FERTILITY; PROPHECY; PROTECTION; SEAGULLS; SWANS; THE GEMSTONES JET, MALACHITE, AND AMBER (HIS GIFT TO HUMANS).

Oannes/Oanes/Oen—Babylon, Phoenicia, and Syria. A god of fertility who lived on land during the day but went into the sea at night, he was believed to have come from the Red Sea bringing the gifts of art and law to humans. In Babylon he was also a god of wisdom. Befitting an old man of the depths, his underwater palace was in the west, toward the setting sun. *Associations:* ABUNDANCE, FERTILITY, WISDOM, THE CONSTELLATION AQUARIUS, ZODIAC SIGN CAPRICORN.

---

59 Robert Blumetti, *The Book of Balder Rising*, 178.

Oceanus/Oceanos/Okeanos—Greece. One of the Titans, a son of Gaia and Ouranos. He was the ruler of the seas. The Greeks worshipped him as a father of both gods and humans. His children with wife/sister Tethys were sea and river nymphs.

Oegir—Norway. A sea god whose name evolved into the word *ogre* to fit his countenance.

Olokun—Nigeria (Yoruba). A sea god and son of Yemanja.

Paikea—Polynesia. The god of sea monsters. In some legends, Paikea is also the name of a whale.

Panope—Greece. One of the Nereids who was invoked by sailors in trouble on stormy seas. Her name means "a wide view over a calm expanse of water," or more literally, "level surface."[60]

Phorcus—Greece. A sea god who represented the white seafoam. He was said to be the keeper or leader of sea monsters. Sources differ on his parentage: Oceanus and Tethys or Poseidon and Amphitrite. He was the father of the Gorgons.

Pontus / Pontos—Greece and Phoenicia. He represented the deep sea. With Gaia (earth) he fathered Nereus and other sea deities as well as monsters.

Portumnus / Portunus—Italy (Roman). A sea god who protected harbors, shores, and shipwrecked sailors. He was known as Palaemon by the Greeks. The Isthmian games were held in his honor. *Association:* DOLPHINS.

Poseidon—Greece. One of the Olympian gods and king of the sea. His parents were Cronos and Rhea. With his brothers, Zeus and Hades, he divided the world so that each could rule a separate part, sky, underworld, and sea, but together they ruled the land. His wife was the sea nymph Amphitrite, but he had many children by a number of women—divine and mortal. A major temple dedicated to him was located on the Cape Sunium jetty overlooking the Aegean. Poseidon was considered tempera-

---

60 Merritt Hughes and A. S. P. Woodhouse, *A Variorum Commentary on the Poems of John Milton*, 669.

mental, the cause of earthquakes and sea storms. The trident was his symbol of power. *Associations:* BULLS, HORSES.

Proteus—Greece. A shepherd of sea creatures, mainly seals who were referred to as his cattle. Also known as Old Man of the Sea,[61] he was a shape-shifter who resided in the deep. *Associations:* PROPHECY, TRANSFORMATION.

Ran—Norway. A sea goddess who was sister and wife of Aegir. With her magic net, she kidnapped sailors from ships and took them to her coral cave. She represented the "stormy spirit of the sea" and "reflected the shifting moods of the ocean."[62] Sailors wore a gold earring in her honor and, if necessary, threw it into the sea as a gift for her to quell a storm. The phrase *Fara til Râna* (go to Ran) means "to drown."[63] *Association:* GOLD.

Riu-to—Japan. A sea god who dwelled at the bottom of the ocean.

Ruhahatu—Polynesia. A sea god of the Society Islands.

Sagara—India. A Hindu sea god.

Salacia—Italy. The goddess of saltwater and wife of Neptune. She was the Roman equivalent of Amphitrite.

Scotia—Cyprus. A sea goddess whose name means "dark one."[64]

Sea Mither—Scotland (Orkney Islands). A sea mother personifying life, summer, and warmth.

Sedna—Canada (Inuit). A darker version of the Alaskan Nerrivik. She was abandoned by her mortal parents and came to represent the dangerous aspects of the sea. Called the Mistress of Life and Death,[65] she pulled those lost at sea down to her realm. She also directed the aquatic migration of fish and seals and was called on in times of famine to let a certain

---

61 Charles Gayley, *The Classic Myths in English Literature*, 86.

62 Cotterell and Storm, *Ultimate Encyclopedia of Mythology*, 189.

63 Bassett, *Legends and Superstitions*, 68.

64 Jobes, *Dictionary of Mythology*, 1408.

65 Hartley Alexander, *North American Mythology*, 6.

number of animals be hunted by humans. When her taboos were not observed, Sedna could cause sea storms. She is also known as Arnarkusaga or Arnakuagsak in Greenland. *Associations:* ABUNDANCE, PROVIDENCE, NATURE.

Shony / Shoney—Scotland (the Hebrides). A sea god who was celebrated at Hallow-tide and known as Leader of the Blue Men. Until the mid-1600s, fishermen made offerings to him for a good catch. Ale was offered to him to bring kelp ashore to use as fertilizer on the fields. *Association:* SAMHAIN.

Sidon—Phoenicia. A version of Poseidon.

Sirens—Greece and Italy. Sea nymphs whose magical songs enchanted sailors and lured them off course. Odysseus had himself strapped to the mast of his ship so he could not respond to their music. The Sirens were venerated on the southwest coast of Italy, where they were known by the names of Ligea (harmony), Leucothea (white), and Parthenope (Virgin Face).[66]

Susa-no-wa—Japan. A mischievous god of sea, storms, and the underworld whose shrine was located at Susa. Some scholars also note him as a moon god.

Suvarnamacha—Thailand. The Siamese queen of the sea, portrayed as a mermaid.

Taaruatai—Polynesia. A sea god of the Society Islands.

Tamayorihime—Japan. A sea goddess who ruled all waters and healing. *Associations:* CLEANSING, CHILDBIRTH, HEALING.

Tamti—Assyria (Chaldean). A primordial mother goddess and a version of Tiamat who was personified by the sea. She was considered a sovereign goddess and was known as the Lady of the Lower Abyss.[67]

---

66 Bassett, *Legends and Superstitions*, 16.
67 François Lenormant, *Chaldean Magic*, 116.

Tangaroa—Polynesia. A sea and sky god who was considered the "supreme creator"[68] in Tahiti and Samoa.

Tawhiri-matea—Polynesia. A sea god of the Society Islands.

Tegid Voel—Wales. The god of the undersea realm and husband of the powerful goddess Cerridwen.

Tethra—Ireland. A sea god and Fomorian king.

Tethys—Greece. A goddess whose consort and brother was Oceanus. She was queen of the sea and mother of a plethora of minor deities called the Oceanides.

Thaumas—Greece. A sea god who personified the reflective quality of water. Nereus and Doris were his parents.

Thetis—Greece. Sea nymph daughter of Nereus and Doris. She was shunned by the amorous Zeus and Poseidon because of the prophecy that she would bear a son who would be greater than his father. She married the mortal King Peleus and bore him a son, Achilles. Thetis was invoked by sailors in trouble. *Associations:* DOLPHINS, ROCK CRYSTAL, SINGING, SPINNING, TRANSFORMATION, WEAVING.

Tiamat—Mesopotamia. The primeval mother personified by the "turbulent, saltwater ocean"[69] that mixed with Apsu, fresh water, which resulted in the creation of the world and a multitude of gods. Because she represented chaos—the wild, feminine side of nature—she was depicted as a dragon or sea monster. The land of Tiamat *(mat tamtim)* was believed to have covered the area of Sumer.

Tien-How—China. A sea goddess of sailors, who venerated her with shrines aboard their ships.

Tritons—Greece. Sea deity children of Poseidon and Amphitrite. They accompanied their father and served as heralds. The Tritons were depicted as half men, half fish with tridents and large whelk shells that they used

---

68 Jobes, *Dictionary of Mythology*, 1531–1532.
69 Cotterell and Storm, *Ultimate Encyclopedia of Mythology*, 326.

as trumpets, controlling the waves with their music. Some sources say that there was only one son, whose name was Triton, rather than many Tritons.

Tuoletan—Finland. One of the chief sea deities.

Ukupanio—Hawaii. A sea deity in the form of a shark who could help or hinder fishermen by herding fish.

Ungal-a-abba—Assyria (Chaldean). A king of the sea and protective god who was celebrated in a hymn that spoke of "sublime waters, holy waters," collected in "the holy and pure ocean."[70]

Vira-Cocha—Peru. A minor god associated with Mama Cocha. His name means "seafoam."

Vourukasha—Iran. A sea deity whose name means "wide gulfed."[71]

Wachilt—Britain. A sea witch and mother of Weyland Smith, the last human who was able to craft magic swords.

Wata-tsumi—Japan. A sea god who possessed two magic gems that controlled the ebb and flow of the tides.

Wata-tsumi-no-kami—Japan (Shinto). A sea god of creation myth.

Weenemäuta—Finland. Queen of the sea.

Ween Kummingas—Finland. King of the sea.

Wellamo / Vellamo—Finland. A sea goddess and wife of Ahti. Her name means "to rock oneself."[72]

Yemanja—Nigeria (Yoruba). A sea goddess and patron spirit of fishermen whose traditions were carried to the New World, where she was also worshipped in Cuba and Brazil. Part of the Candomble religious and healing tradition, she was considered the ocean's spirit. Yemanja was depicted adorned with a crescent moon, walking on the waves. In Brazil on New Year's Eve, altars dedicated to her were built on the beaches. *Associations:* COWRY SHELLS, DIVINATION, DREAMS, PROSPERITY, NEW YEAR'S DAY.

---

70 François Lenormant, *Chaldean Magic*, 184.

71 Jobes, *Dictionary of Mythology*, 1659.

72 Ibid., 1672.

Yemanja

Yen Kung—China. A god of waves and wind who was believed to have sent a tidal wave to protect Shanghai from pirates in the sixteenth century.

Yuqiang—China. A god of the sea and ocean winds. With the help of fifteen turtles, he anchored the five floating islands.

JOURNAL QUESTIONS

1. Do you think that myths serve any purpose for us in today's world? Why or why not?

2. If you were a navigator in ancient times, would you have searched for the "Hidden Lands," the otherworldly place just out of view?

3. Are you drawn to learn more about a particular saint, deity, or pantheon? Which?

4. Do you feel that working with the energy of a saint or deity might help or enhance your connection with the ocean's energy and ultimately further your inner journey? How?

III

ALTARS, TOOLS,
AND DIVINATION

So comes to us at times, from the unknown
And inaccessible solitudes of being,
The rushing of the sea-tides of the soul;
And inspirations, that we deem our own,
Are some divine foreshadowing and foreseeing
Of things beyond our reason or control.

HENRY WADSWORTH LONGFELLOW
The Sound of the Sea

WHEN WORKING WITH ENERGY IN meditation, prayer, or ritual, our experience is enhanced if we have a meaningful place for it, a place set aside from our everyday lives. The concept of the altar dates to that prehistoric time when people began making offerings to their deities and needed a special place in which to do it. While altars and their purposes have evolved over the millennia, they continue to fulfill a fundamental need that goes beyond one's specific spiritual orientation.

An altar has a certain power because it is not just a thing that holds a collection of objects. Intention and energy transform it into a space that transcends the mundane level of our world. When we use an altar, we step outside the boundaries of our everyday lives. When we sit in front of it, we open our hearts and psyches to the larger questions that guide our souls. Not only do we look for the meaning of life, we also seek ways to bring meaning into our lives.

As a central part of ritual and worship, an altar is a place of spiritual encounter. It reminds us of our contact with the divine as well as our contact with our inner soul. Through meditation we seek to explore our interior life; to go beyond the mind and find our essential, true self. Earlier we noted Eckhart Tolle's distinction between our physical-world "mind" and our inner-self "being." This "being" consciousness is the true self, not the outer world of "doing." As Dr. Wayne Dyer noted, this is why we call ourselves human beings and not human doings.[1]

Using an altar strikes a familiar chord within us. We may not understand why, but we sense a shift in energy away from ordinary awareness.

---

1 Dyer, *Power of Intention,* 155.

Altars hold objects of inspiration and devotion, creating a space that is visibly and energetically linked to the spiritual and physical worlds. The altar provides clues to our innermost thoughts and feelings. The Greek word *gnosis* is usually translated as "knowledge," but it can also mean "insight." According to Elaine Pagels, "gnosis involves an intuitive process of knowing oneself."[2] An altar becomes a tool for gnosis—knowledge that comes from spiritual insight and self-illumination. The things that we place on an altar come to symbolize what is going on in our hearts and minds. When we work with the energy of sea deities and saints, creating a special type of altar helps us connect with the ocean's power on a personal level.

Sea Altars

A sea altar can be as simple or elaborate as you like. My main altar is constantly morphing: like the tides' ebb and flow, it has its own rhythm. For a while I might add items until it resembles the shore at low tide strewn with a plethora of shells and other flotsam and jetsam that I find on the beach. When the balance tips and the energy flow isn't right, I remove things—occasionally down to the bare tabletop, where I start with one shell or seagull feather and let it evolve again. It is never the same for long.

Whenever we go to the beach to meditate, pray, or to simply be, Nancy Cunningham suggests making a "found" altar with the objects you find on the shore that day. Begin by drawing a circle in the sand to define your altar, or use kelp to mark the space. (Look for loose kelp at the high-tide line. While kelp beds may be accessible at low tide, don't pull off kelp that is attached to rocks.) As you find things such as seashells, stones, sea glass, or feathers, take a moment to hold each item. Get a sense of its energy and where to place it on your altar. In addition to the kelp, be mindful to not disturb other living things. If you pick up shells from tidal pools, check to see if they are occupied. If they are, handle them gently and return them to where you found them. Sea creatures such as

---

2 Elaine Pagels, *Gnostic Gospels*, xix.

periwinkles and limpets hunker down and wait for the tide's return in these pools. If they are moved to an area where the tide cannot reach them, they will die.

If you create a temporary altar below the high-tide line, you can leave it as a gift for Mother Ocean, but make sure that everything you leave behind is natural. Depart with the intention of sending love and healing energy to the sea and to the natural world at large.

If you find a grouping of objects that seem to have been arranged by human hands, leave it alone. Another person may have placed them there with a special purpose. To move or take any item is to interfere with that energy. Have respect, no matter how appealing an object may be to you.

While shell gathering is a fun pursuit—and for some of us an obsession—once in a while you may find something too beautiful to touch. A particular shell may look gorgeous resting against a rock, or a scatter of shells may seem like a still life of perfection. When this occurs, live in the moment. Fully and deeply appreciate the gift; it is a gift to merely behold true simple beauty. It will remain in your memory all the more wonderful for never having been spoiled. Such an experience may occur in a flash, but it will stay with you long after.

For an indoor sea altar, consider these suggestions.

If you use candles, choose ones in sea colors—shades of blue, green, and white, which can represent seafoam as well as the cleansing aspect of the ocean. For tapers, I sprinkle a little sea salt in the bottom of the candleholders before placing a new one in to provide a connection with the ocean. Any scented candle you use in your sea-centering practice is good at other times on your altar, too, because your mind will immediately go to that frame of reference.

In addition to seashells and candles, the other items mentioned for sea centering function well on altars: pictures of the ocean; vessels of water, salt, and sand; found objects. Images or figurines of sea deities can also help forge your link with the ocean's energy. A depiction of a sea creature that resonates with you may also be appropriate. (In section V we will discuss "sea fetches." An image of this totemic sea creature is a natural for your sea altar.)

Sea glass is particularly relevant on an altar that is used for healing meditation. Although the glass is not originally from the ocean, it has been touched and transformed by it. Its broken, sharp edges have been softened and it has become a thing of beauty—as do we, with the effects of Mother Ocean.

Whether you are creating a temporary altar or a more permanent one in your home, choose items with personal and spiritual meaning for you. Listen to your intuition and they will be right for you.

While I have seashells on my altar, I also keep formal collections of them elsewhere in my home—which, I have to admit, are more to ooh and aah over than anything else. In addition to these, I set aside other small areas (seashell shrines, if you will) in my house and garden. They serve as reminders of my faith and my inner journey as I go about my everyday activities. In addition, it's probably no surprise that the logo for my business is the image of a seashell.

SEASHELLS AS TOOLS

The most natural, and obvious, tool for Sea Magic is the seashell. On the most basic level, you really only need one shell to hold sea water, but additional ones on your altar can help boost energy and serve other functions, too. And they do not have to be extravagant or exotic specimens. As you will see, even a broken shell can hold wonderful energy. Follow your intuition for what is appropriate for you. Let's look at some ideas for shells as tools. (See section IV for details on specific shells.)

As a water vessel, a scallop, clam, or cockle shell works well. So does a chambered nautilus, placed in a shell stand that holds it securely with the opening pointing up. This idea has been around for a long time: eighteenth-century goldsmiths created elaborate chalices from nautilus shells.[3] But as an altar vessel it is needlessly large. In addition, the nautilus is somewhat endangered, so unless you already happen to have one I would not recommend getting it for this purpose.

---

3 R. Tucker Abbott, *Kingdom of the Seashell*, 193.

Shells can also hold sand or sea salt; consider a scallop, clam, mussel, or cockle. If you find a complete shell with its hinge ligament intact, it can be used for a unique presentation of other small shells.

Although some shells may seem extremely delicate, most are rather tough. They have to be to prevent attacks from predators and to withstand the constant knockabout in the tides. Many of them handle heat well and can serve nicely as incense burners. (Be sure to set them on a heat-resistant tile or surface before lighting.) I have a six-inch-wide clamshell that I frequently use for this purpose. When it's not in service on my altar, it sits the other way around on a table in my living room. It's a beautiful and simple shell, but if you pick it up and turn it over you see the blackened area on its inner surface.

Consider letting shells represent the compass points on your altar: navigating the seas requires knowledge of the directions. Certain shells are especially suitable.

Shells for the Cardinal Directions

West: Represents dusk and the element water. Water is a force that shapes our physical world and symbolically cleanses our souls. Use a shell with the colors of the setting sun or one filled with water.

North: Represents night and the element earth. Earth is the solid foundation of our world. Use a dark-colored moon shell, a sand dollar, or a starfish. Unlike fish and other ocean dwellers, these critters spend their time in contact with the earth on the ocean floor.

East: Represents dawn and the element air. Air is the breath of life. Use shells the color of the rising sun. A yellow or pink scallop can represent radiant beams of light. Alternatively, jingle shells are delicate and light as a breeze.

South: Represents midday and the element fire. Fire is the spark of spirit that burns within us and connects us with the Divine. Use a white clam shell the color of the noonday sun which can also serve as an incense burner.

Seashells can be used in the same way crystals and gemstones are used, and vice-versa. Coral and pearls, too, can be used in place of shells.

Many legends note that magic mirrors were used by undines and mermaids. Gluing seashells or sea glass around a mirror frame is a way to create a scrying tool. However, that is about as far as I would suggest going with "decorating" items for Sea Magic. I agree with Veronica Parker Johns, who noted that seashells don't have to "do something or be done unto rather than merely being allowed to be."[4] After all, we find them on the *bea*ch. They simply are, and that is their beauty and power.

Shells offer potent visual symbols, too. The round single-shelled mollusks that sport a spiral design—such as the Moon Snail (*Polinices duplicatus*), Giant Sundial (*Architectonica maxima*), Ram's Horn (*Marisa cornuarietis*), and Common Periwinkle (*Littorina littorea*)—are particularly relevant on a sea altar. The spiral is one of the oldest and most enduring symbols of the Great Mother Goddess. On a seashell, of course, it represents Mother Ocean.

The yoni symbol of female (pro)creative power has been linked with the cowry shell (*Cypraea moneta* or *C. annulus*) since ancient times. Shells that represent male energy include the Florida Horse Conch (*Pleuroploca gigantean*), Crown Conch (*Melongena corona*) with its strong bull-like horns, and the giant Eastern Murex (*Hexaplex fulvescens*). A Pink Conch, also called a Queen Conch (*Strombus gigas*), and a Horse or a Crown Conch together on an altar represent the balance of male and female energies.

PRACTICE: SEASHELL CLEANSINGS AND BLESSINGS

As with anything used for a spiritual or healing purpose, shells should be cleansed to remove any unwanted energy and empower them with desired energy. Even a shell pulled directly from the surf should be cleansed: not only does this remove old energy, but we also imbue it with our intentions. We can do this with wet or dry cleansing methods.

If you can take your shells to a beach, you can do a real "on-site" Wave Blessing, spoken as you stand in the water. Simply wade in far enough

---

4 Veronica Parker Johns, *She Sells Seashells*, 187.

Goddess statue with cowries, moons, and other shells

that you can distinguish separate waves as they come ashore. You need not go far. The big breakers do not have to crash over you and your shells; the smaller and gentler waves closer to shore do nicely. If you have a number of little shells, you may want to place them in a small mesh laundry bag to prevent loss.

The Wave Blessing

Stand at the tide line and begin by saying:

"Mother Ocean, I call on you to bless these shells."

Dip them into the water of three successive waves, saying one of the following lines for each wave:

"Mother Ocean, cleanse these with your foam."

"Mother Ocean, purify these with your salt."

"Mother Ocean, charge these with your magic."

Cup the shells in your hands and close your eyes. Take a few long, deep breaths and feel the power of the sea. End with:

"Mother Ocean, thank you for your flow of blessings."

When I used the Wave Blessing at the beach for my set of divination cowries, I was pleasantly surprised by a shell washing right into my hands on the third wave. Even though it is a broken and battered whelk, I have kept this gift on my altar ever since. I treasure the astonishing manner and timing by which it came to me.

If it is winter and you are not a polar bear, or if you live inland, the Wave Blessing can be performed at home. Collect or prepare enough seawater in which to dip your shells, and place it in a bowl. Ask Mother Ocean for her blessing and then, after each of the three calls to her in the Wave Blessing, dip the shells into the water. Although there will not be waves in your bowl of water, simply pause between each dipping. If you have a recording of ocean sounds, you can use that to cue your dips. If you are consecrating larger shells that don't dunk easily into a bowl, simply dip your fingers into the water and sprinkle it over the shells. End by thanking Mother Ocean.

If you prefer, a dry blessing can be done by sprinkling sea salt over the shells as you follow the blessing sequence. Once you have used the salt this way, gather it into a jar. At the next full moon, place the jar outside or on a window sill where it will be bathed in moonlight as you use the Moon Blessing. The salt can be reused afterward.

Moon Blessing of Salt

As you set the jar of salt in the moonlight, say:
"Sister Moon, shining bright,
As you guide the tides this night,
Purify this salt for me
With the magic of the sea."

A note on purchasing seashells: shells that you find yourself are wonderfully gratifying because they seem like personal gifts from Mother Ocean. But if you can't get to a beach, or if you would like something that you cannot find yourself, the remedy is—shopping! One drawback, however, is that the majority of shell shops tend to be in coastal areas, which is not very helpful if you are inland. The solution to this problem is shopping online, but of course, there are pros and cons.

The advantage of shopping in a store is that not only can you see exactly what you are buying, but you can hold it and sense its energy. I bought a beautiful volute in a shop in Milan, Italy, based on how it felt in my hands. As for the Internet, I have used it to purchase a few shells that I would not have been able to get otherwise. I have, for the most part, had good results. As with anything that is purchased online, it's good idea to check the merchant's return policy before ordering.

It is important to know this about shells from the commercial trade: finding beautifully intact seashells is not left to chance. Mollusks and other sea creatures are taken alive and killed. Because of this, if you choose to buy shells it is important not only to do an energy cleansing, but also to thank the creature that created the shell and lost its life because of it. Above all, treat it with respect.

A Word about Sand

A dish of sand on the altar can be used to draw Norse runes, the Celtic Ogham, or other symbols, or to simply run your fingers through. Sand itself is beautiful and carries with it the power of the ages. Composed mainly of rock that has been weathered and pulverized over the millennia and transported to the sea, beach sand is infinitely variable. Most sand consists of quartz and feldspar.[5] Quartz is the most common and widely dispersed mineral on earth; it is physically hard and chemically stable. Its commonness belies its power as a transformer that amplifies and focuses energy.

Quartz is not the only mineral to be found in a handful of sand: pink and red garnet, black tourmaline, and beryl are also common. The sparkly flakes are usually mica. Tiny grains also come from seashells and coral as well as silicified wood, a component of the "singing sands" on the island of Eigg in the Inner Hebrides.[6] Acoustic sands exist in a number of places around the world. Some of their sounds have been described as singing, barking, and whistling, as well as booming. There is no definitive scientific explanation for these sounds, despite numerous theories

---

5 Orrin Pilkey, Tracy Rice, and William Neal, *How to Read a North Carolina Beach*, 29.

6 Rachel Carson, *The Edge of the Sea*, 129.

about the sand grains' size, shape, and silica content, and the air spaces between the grains.

Gather a handful of sand and take a good look at it. You'll find that the grains vary in color, size, and shape. They can be large and easy to distinguish or incredibly small and fine. While the individual components of a handful of sand may vary in color, the overall cast of a beach may be generally light, dark, or a specific color.

It took ages to reduce rocks and minerals to granular size and carry them to the beach where you found them. Allow your imagination to fathom this journey through time and place. Appreciate the beauty of the sand and the mighty forces that brought these grains together.

A beach constantly evolves as the land and ocean seek a level of equilibrium. Sand is the mediator of that in-between world, as wind and wave re-contour the shoreline. For a time the beach belongs to the land, but as the tide turns it is once again claimed by Mother Ocean. Sand carries the energy of this movement and the perpetual cycles of tides and seasons.

PRACTICE: CREATING A SEA CIRCLE OF ENERGY

While an altar is the physical manifestation of your intent to create sacred space, making or casting a circle builds energy for sacred space. The circle is one of humankind's oldest and most elemental symbols, our greatest representation of perfection and wholeness, integrity and endlessness, unity and completion. It echoes the turning and returning cycles of life, of the seasons, of time and timelessness. It shows us that all events, all life, and everything in the universe are connected in a perpetual flow of energy. When we make a circle, we are creating a special and powerful space—a space where our energies become focused and strengthened; a place where we share in the mysteries of body, mind, and spirit, of time and eternity.

A sacred circle is created by energetically defining an area. We can call on the four directions or elements, if we wish, or we can call on just one element—water being the key element for Sea Magic. The practice outlined below shows both options: one that invokes the directions by way of four of the earth's seas, and a simpler version that does not refer to the four cardinal points.

The physical space of your circle can encompass an entire room or surround just you and your altar. To begin, have some seawater on hand, then close your eyes and take a few deep breaths to center your energy. When you are ready, open your eyes and create your circle using any of the methods presented here—or craft your own.

Dip your fingertips into your seawater, then sprinkle it along the way as you define your circle. If you are indoors, you can place a seashell—half a scallop, clam, or mussel—at each cardinal point to sprinkle water into, or simply carry the seawater as you walk the perimeter of your circle. Alternatively, you could sprinkle a tiny amount of sea salt to define the circle, then sweep it up afterward. (If you do this, discard the salt by burying it in the ground or in a flowerpot of soil, or take it to a beach. Because it was used for a spiritual purpose, the salt should not be tossed away in the garbage. Additionally, I would not recommend reusing the salt—even after the Moon Blessing—because on the floor it may have mixed with other particles such as dust or pet fur, which would not be appropriate for cleansing work.)

If you are doing your work on a beach, simply draw a circle in the sand as you speak the words. The words offered here are merely suggestions to help you get started. If calling on a particular goddess or Mother Mary is more appropriate for you, do so. It is essential that the words flow naturally from your heart.

Creating a Sea Circle of Energy

To invoke the four directions in your circle: with your jar or shell of seawater, move around the cardinal points at the boundary of your circle. Beginning with west, sprinkle seawater on the floor or into a shell for that direction as you say the first line of the invocation. Then move clockwise to the north, east, and south as you say the subsequent lines. Say:

"Vastness of the Pacific,
Power of the Atlantic,
Strength of the Mediterranean,
Calm of the Sargasso."

Place the jar or shell of water on your altar and say:

"Spirit of the seas, Mother Ocean,
I call on you to bless this circle with your presence.
As the sea encircles the earth,
So too you hold this space sacred.
Tenet mare sal sapientia."
(The sea holds the salt of wisdom.)

For a simpler approach without the four directions, use these alternate words:

"Mother Ocean, Mother Ocean
Bring your pure energy;
Cleanse this space for my purpose
With the power of the sea."

or:

"Power of ocean, power of sea,
Cleanse and purify this space for me."

The next time you do a sea centering, meditate, pray, or simply sit in silence, create a sea circle and note whether it makes a difference for you. Creating a circle also helps prepare you energetically and mentally for your purpose. It aids in focusing the mind for your intent and provides time to make the transition from the outer world to inner space.

When you are finished with the circle after your meditation, sea centerings, or other energy work, dissolve it and return the space to the everyday level of energy. If you are more comfortable addressing and dismissing each cardinal direction individually, do so; however, it is not necessary. If you are using a candle, blow it out when you finish the words for dissolving a sea circle. Take a moment or two to visualize your circle dissolving like the remnants of a wave roiling then flattening into calmness as it recedes. Become aware of your feet planted firmly on land as you return to an everyday level of energy.

Dissolving a Sea Circle

"Circle ebb like tide to source;
Mother Ocean, guide my course."

Even though you dissolve the circle, engaging the energy in this way enhances your physical altar. The objects we consider sacred become so because of our intent and energy. Some of the energy we raise remains with the altar, further empowering it, which in turn further empowers us when we return to meditate or do other work. Over time, an altar becomes a very special and personal place. It may physically evolve as objects are added or taken away, but the power remains and develops. Making and using an altar is a creative process, a work always in progress. It is part of our spiritual journey and as such it is the ever-changing scenery along our path.

ORACULAR GUIDANCE AND SIGNS

Except for the requisite sound-bite horoscopes in daily newspapers and websites, oracular arts are not part of modern society. In fact, they are often treated with suspicion and mistrust. Yet the spiritual side of the self seems to have a profound need for guidance by something wiser, as Dianne Skafte has noted.[7]

Some shells come to us as gifts, like the one that came into my hand during a Wave Blessing. And sometimes they even come to us as oracles: I believe I have experienced this myself with two sand dollars. Soon after I moved to Maine, I was walking along a rocky beach where few entirely intact shells could be found. I was surprised when a delicate little sand dollar washed up to my feet. It was complete and whole. At the time I was making a major transition in my life and interpreted Mother Ocean's gift as a sign that I was coming through these changes as intact as the sand dollar. I recalled the previous time I had found one, three years earlier. Unsettled with my life, I was spending time near the ocean in preparation for my pilgrimage to Ireland. The little sand dollar I found that day was intact on the bottom, but the top side had a large hole in the middle. Not until later did I realize that the first sand dollar, too, represented me: My center, my heart, had been missing; I was not doing what I wanted to do,

7 Dianne Skafte, *Listening to the Oracle*, 2.

what I felt I was meant to do. The pilgrimage changed me, and now, three years later, I was beginning a whole new life. This was more confirmation than guidance in the classical sense, but it was a sublime experience nonetheless.

Keep in mind that not every shell we find is an oracular message. Actually, few are, but let us be in tune with our souls enough to know when we are receiving a sign or simply a lovely gift. Meanings may not be clear at first. We may wait a long while until the time is right and we are ready to receive the information. When a sign becomes clear, the next step is trust. Decide whether you accept it by listening to your intuition. Examine whether your heart-of-hearts tells you the sign is valid. If it is, surrender to the experience of the universe communicating with you.

Oracular signs or guidance are never forceful; they are merely presented. We may or may not notice them and we can choose whether to accept them. If at any time you feel pushed, rushed, fearful, or expected to do something uncomfortable, something else is going on. Stop and check your motives (or someone else's) and take time to examine what you are feeling as well as the source of anything untoward. Oracular signs are positive and serve to deepen our spiritual well-being.

Throughout the ages thousands of divination methods have been devised and employed—from the famed Oracle of Delphi to the humble fortune cookie. You name it and people have tried it. Levity and playfulness have their place in practices with sacred roots, but with any endeavor at divination, sincerity and mindfulness are the key ingredients. The goal of divination is to unite the personal with the mystical; the mundane with the sacred. Truth is of utmost importance.

PRACTICE: DIVINATION WITH COWRY SHELLS

One seashell divination system originated with Santeria, an Afro-Cuban spiritual practice that blends Catholicism with the magical and religious beliefs of the Yoruba people of Nigeria. The Yoruba saw a correlation between their gods, *orishas*, and Christian saints. The shell known as the Money Cowry is used in this complex system, which is called the Diloggun.[8] Because the cowry shell is considered a mouthpiece of the gods, this practice is a sacred one. The Diloggun is used in two ways: to reveal an overview of a person's life and its problem areas, both general and specific, and to point a person toward a solution.

Although the form of seashell divination presented in this book employs cowries, it is not the Diloggun. The method described here was created to provide a simpler practice (using only nine cowries instead of sixteen) and it is not specific to any particular religion. Nine shells are used as an amplified sacred number (three times three) and based on the attributes and associations found in numerology rather than Christian proverbs, as is the Diloggun.

Seashell divination is concerned not only with seeking truth, but with bringing truth to a situation. It is intended to help us live our individual truth by learning more about who we are. In the words of the Oracle of Delphi, "Know thyself."

Preparing the Cowries

As with a coin toss, any divinatory object needs to have a fair chance of landing one way or the other without ambiguity. Because cowry shells have a rounded side, they need to be cut to avoid rolling. While it would seem easier to use a flat shell like a scallop, I like the symbolism of the cowry as an oracular mouthpiece, which is only one of its sacred associations. (Refer to section IV for more information about cowries.)

To cut a cowry shell, Migene González-Wippler suggests making an indentation at one end of the shell's rounded side.[9] A file, knife blade,

---

8 Migene González-Wippler, *Seashell Divination*, 5–6.

9 Ibid., 10.

These cowries show a natural serrated opening (right)
and a wide hand-cut opening (left).

or the tip of a pair of scissors can then be used to remove the rounded belly portion from the shell. As someone who is not exactly agile doing things like this and because I value my fingers, I find it safer to buy pre-cut shells. These are available very inexpensively in some shell shops and through the Internet.

The cut shells have a wide opening where the belly was removed and a natural, narrow, serrated opening on the opposite side: that "mouth-piece" side is the one we count when tossing the shells.

The shells should be cleansed before they are used, especially since they are for divination purposes. Use one of the cleansing methods described on pages 58–60, or spread a layer of sea salt on a plate, lay the shells on the salt either side up, then set the plate outside or on a windowsill where it will be bathed in the light of the full moon. In this way the shells are re-attuned to Mother Ocean and to the power of Sister Moon who holds sway over the tides. Or if you have another way of cleansing and preparing sacred objects, follow what works best for you.

Once the cowries have been prepared, you may want to dedicate the set of shells to a particular sea deity, to the Holy Mother, or to your intent for a higher purpose. You may want to inscribe a symbol on the shells

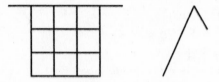

Left: The Celtic Ogham Mór. Right: The Norse rune Lagu.

or on the bag or box in which you keep them. These can be inscribed with ink or paint or simply scratched onto the surface of the shell with a pin. Symbols can include astrological signs, the Norse runes, or the Celtic Ogham. (The latter two systems with their meanings are outlined in appendix B.)

I have found the Ogham symbol Mór to be a powerful reminder of Sea Magic for me because of my return to the sea while on pilgrimage in Ireland. It is usually called Amhancholl and, like all the other symbols in the Celtic tree alphabet, it is associated with trees (pine and witch hazel). However, unlike the other Oghams, it has this alternate name and connection with the sea. The character itself resembles a fishing net. *Mór* is the Old Irish word for the sea.[10] It suggests ancient wisdom that is available especially when the moon and tides are full. If you prefer a Norse rune, you might be drawn to Lagu, which is associated with the sea and the unending depths of the ocean. In any case, the use of symbols on the shells or their container is a personal decision and not necessary for their function.

Throwing the Cowries

Place a soft cloth on a table or the floor where you are doing a reading. As you prepare your space, give thought to what you want to clarify in your life. Know your purpose and intent for throwing the cowries. When you are ready, begin by holding the shells in one hand in front of your heart. If you are doing a reading for yourself, go through a brief sea centering as you hold them. When doing a reading for someone else, do the centering

10 John Michael Greer, *The New Encyclopedia of the Occult*, 313.

beforehand and then have the other person hold the shells at their heart center. You may also want to coach the other person to close their eyes and take a few slow, deep breaths.

You will throw the shells three times. First shake them in your hand as you would a set of dice (or have the other person do this), then gently release them onto the cloth, again like dice. Count the number of shells that fall with the serrated "oracle mouthpiece" up. Gather all of them and then throw them two more times, noting each time how many land serrated side up. The number from the first throw is the issue or life aspect that is calling for attention. The numbers from the second and third throws complement the first, supporting or further explaining it. In addition, these can point to a solution for a potential problem.

If all three throws produce the same number, perhaps you need to examine one life aspect from several angles. For example, on each of the three tosses, four of the shells landed with their serrated sides up, as shown here. The number four is concerned with community, so this is the life aspect you would want to examine closely. (A full explanation of each life aspect is given below.) If you have recently moved to a new area, the cowries could be suggesting that you get out and meet people to build a new network. If you have not moved house, have a look at the order and stability in your life outside of the family circle. Are you are grounded and taking part in social activities? Do you have a network of people to rely on? If you are not integrated into some form of community you may want to examine why not.

For a successful reading, we must be completely honest with ourselves. If we see that we have been wrong about something or behaved in a way that was not mindful or responsible, we need to examine how to put things right. But we should not get angry or upset with ourselves over any such realization. That was not the point of the reading and would be counterproductive for the process. Learning how to apologize, if necessary, and how to alter our current way of thinking or behaving is the first step in making positive changes in our lives.

The interpretation of a reading will depend on the current situation and the intent or question in mind at the outset. Take your time and review your situation. How do you know whether or not you have reached the right conclusion? Examine what your intuition indicates.

Occasionally all the cowries may fall mouthpiece down. If this happens on the first throw, take them all in your hands and hold them to your heart. Take a moment to clear your mind. If you want to deal with a specific question, bring that and how it relates to your life clearly into your mind. For example, if an important test or sporting event is coming up and you are focused on acing or winning it, you may have expected an eight on your first throw (life aspect for achievement). However, you could be barking up the wrong tree thinking that you might get confirmation of a sure win. In this case, a zero may be telling you that your focus is wrong, that you are too wrapped up in something that is not so important in the greater scheme of your life.

Interpreting the Cowries

Let's make a broad survey of each number's meaning and how certain aspects may manifest in our lives.

ONE

Aspect: Self

Associations: Beginnings, creativity, independence, individuality, isolation, leadership, loneliness, originality, willpower.

As individuals we can choose to assert our independence and uniqueness as well as our willpower and determination to stand out from the crowd. In addition, we can use our strong personality in a positive manner to become an inspiring leader. However, when the ego is out of balance, single-mindedness and stubbornness can result from a negative use of our will. This can lead to isolation and loneliness. But the number one is also about beginnings. We have the capacity to pick up the pieces and start over when necessary, using that spark of creativity and originality that makes us unique.

TWO

Aspect: Relationships

Associations: Balance, division, duality, harmony, partnership, solidarity, tolerance.

The first step outside of self is a one-on-one relationship with another person. As we form bonds with others we create a web, a network. All relationships, both intimate and casual, require work if we are to strike a balanced partnership. Through understanding, healthy tolerance, and fair compromise we can create harmony and solidarity and foster a relationship that can last a lifetime. When relationships are out of balance, divisions can occur which can become self-perpetuating and cause the relationship to break apart. By tuning in to our intuition and being mutually respectful, shyness or furtiveness can be redirected into a shared level of honesty that can surmount obstacles.

THREE

Aspect: Family

Associations: Abundance, energy, family, fertility, fulfillment, self-expression.

With family comes the need to step up the energy to handle multiple relationships in close quarters. Along with this comes the pursuit of abundance and comfort. Because being part of a family means caring for more than self and one other person, it becomes essential to set and pursue goals that benefit everyone. At times this extroverted energy can get channeled into wasteful and showy materialism. In addition, we may try to go in too many directions at once and end up going nowhere. But family can be a center of strength, support, and fulfillment if we are mindful of how and where we put our energy. With all that goes on in a family, maintaining our own individuality and self-expression, and allowing others to do the same, are essential ingredients in keeping things running smoothly.

A shell toss showing a count of four

FOUR

Aspect: Community

Associations: Dedication, dependability, luck, manifestation, order, reality, stability, strength, truth.

As we continue to move outward from self, we reach the larger world of community. Here is a solid reality check where we can learn about other people and their relationships and families. To have successful community we need to manifest order and stability, which comes about when individuals act with strength and dedication to the common good. Being reliable and holding to the courage of our convictions keep us grounded in truth. Just as families and relationships take work, so too does being in community. Because of community's larger scale, the ball can be dropped and misunderstandings can occur. We may get lost in the crowd; we may lose the shared vision or our own ambition to do our part. Not wanting to go with the herd can cause anger and overreaction. Therefore me must remain mindful of our core beliefs, seek understanding, and act with justice and fairness.

FIVE

Aspect: Purpose in life

Associations: Change, communication, curiosity, freedom, knowledge,
logic, restlessness, search, travel.

It may take time for us to figure out our true calling, and we need the
freedom to follow our curiosity. We may be led to try various careers or
lifestyles. Such experimentation in itself can teach us to become resource-
ful, versatile, and adventurous. But if we seem to need constant change,
if we are always on the move, unwilling to be tied down, we may find
ourselves restless and dissatisfied. Unfocused energy leaves us unful-
filled. The most important ingredient in seeking our life's purpose is to be
truthful to ourselves. Communication with the inner self as well as with
the people around us will open the channels and bring us the knowledge
we need to discover what we truly want to do. Setting a logical course
with optimism will get us where we need and want to be.

SIX

Aspect: Service

Associations: Beauty, devotion, duty, equilibrium, fidelity, love, perfection, service, sympathy, wholeness.

This is a varied aspect; how we perceive it depends on how we perceive
the idea of service. Service can go beyond the concept of doing one's
duty; on a personal level it is concerned with fidelity, devotion, and love.
We may think of these qualities mainly in terms of intimate relationships,
but they can also be applied to a faith, a group, or an ideal. Having and
acting with sympathy can bring equilibrium and wholeness into our own
life and to the lives around us. Still, feeling responsibility to a community
can, if not understood, feel like a burden. It always helps to stop and take
time to assess what we think and feel. Service and the number six are
also associated with beauty and perfection. In medieval Europe, service
was symbolized by a six-petaled rose—which does not exist in nature.
And so the six-petaled rose of service is something to give freely and
from the heart.

SEVEN

Aspect: Spirituality

Associations: The ethereal, faith, introspection, otherworldly realms, religion, spirituality.

The energy center at the top of the head, known as the seventh chakra or crown chakra, connects us to the spiritual and ethereal energy of the universe. We develop this aspect by making time for introspection because we know this is how we gain true insight. If we do, we may find that those around us say that they feel calm in our presence. But if we often choose to step out of the bustling mainstream in order to find that tranquility, we may be misunderstood and perceived as aloof or secretive. At times we may turn from the public eye because of our sensitivity. This requires a balancing act, but in the long run we find that understanding and supportive people come into our lives.

EIGHT

Aspect: Achievement

Associations: Accomplishment, confidence, power, strength, success.

The word *achievement* may at first bring to mind the successful entrepreneur who oozes confidence and power. While confidence is an essential component, setting realistic goals and planning a direct path toward them are also vital to achievement. Having faith both in ourself and in the goal go a long way toward accomplishing what we set out to do. However, when the ambitious pursuit of power and status becomes equal to the original goal, other people—often those close to us—can get hurt as selfishness festers and spreads. Strength and confidence can help us accomplish great things when energy flows from the heart. After all, what is the point of reaching for the stars if we end up there alone?

NINE

Aspect: Higher Self

Associations: Charity, compassion, generosity, healing power, humanitarianism, selflessness.

This is our inner true self that lives in the heart center and is expressed through acts of compassion and healing. Selfless charity and generosity are their own reward when they reflect a genuine interest in helping others. The ability to transform the self to a higher level frequently occurs after we have undergone great difficulty ourself. If we are feeling unstable emotionally, we may be unable to see our way clear for a time; we may be unaware of the gifts we possess. Sometimes the process of healing can be our own greatest guru, helping uncover our highest humanity.

———•———

Seashell divination functions as a tool for exploring our inner world. The aspects of life that come up when we toss the shells are an expression of our intention, whether conscious or subconscious. Whatever our mind is focused on, our energy follows—whether we are aware of it or not. Seashell divination can help bring issues to the surface where we can deal with them or simply keep tabs on what we are feeling. As Dr. Wayne Dyer noted, "feelings are clues."[11]

As we have seen, signs—information that comes to us indirectly—may not be clear to us at first. To understand certain things fully, we need a chance to look back, with a long view if possible. This is where journaling can be invaluable. Nuances fade over time, or we simply forget details. The ability to look back and review previous divination sessions allows us to connect the dots and find meanings that are relevant to our current situations.

---

11 Dyer, *Power of Intention*, 37.

JOURNAL QUESTIONS

1. Whether or not keeping an altar is a new experience for you, how do you feel about the objects you place there?

2. Has creating a sea circle served to amplify the energy of sacred space around your altar? If so, how did it feel—physically, emotionally, spiritually?

3. Do you believe that you have received oracular signs or messages? If so, what were they and how did you differentiate them as signs?

4. Has working with seashell divination helped you focus on specific aspects of your life? Which aspects, and to what extent?

IV
SEASHELLS

*G*ather a shell from the strewn beach
And listen at its lips: they sigh
The same desire and mystery,
The echo of the whole sea's speech.
And all mankind is thus at heart
Not anything but what thou art:
And Earth, Sea, Man, are all in each.

DANTE GABRIEL ROSSETTI
The Sea Limits

AS GIFTS FROM MOTHER OCEAN, seashells offer a tantalizing promise of discovery. Their energy and beauty inspire us, making them perfect aids in Sea Magic. Their legacy of human use dates back thousands of years: in addition to food and medicine, seashells have been used for mundane and sacred purposes worldwide. In Africa, Asia, the Americas, Australia, India, Europe, and the Middle East, ancient peoples used them as kitchen utensils and general household tools, as well as for personal adornment, Still used in jewelry today, shells were major bling for prehistoric people. Archaeological excavations of Neanderthal and Cro-Magnon burials found cockle and cowry shells placed in "mystical patterns around the skulls."[1]

Shells were widely used as currency in trade, as evidenced by cowries from the Indian Ocean found at ancient sites in the caves of Southern France.[2] The Romans used rock shells such as the Purple-dye Murex (*Bolinus brandaris*) and Trunk Murex (*Hexaplex trunculus*) for the rich purple dye "to color imperial and ecclesiastical robes."[3] Scallops were not the only shells picked up on spiritual pilgrimages and kept as sacred relics. When the grave of Bishop Mayhew of Hereford, England, was opened some years after his burial in 1516, mussel and oyster shells were found by his side.[4]

Shells exude energy, and it is no wonder people have long been attracted to them. Their shapes and color patterns suggest flowing movement,

---

1 Abbott, *Shells*, 10.

2 W. J. Perry, *The Origin of Magic and Religion*, 10.

3 Fred Woodward, *Identifying Shells*, 6.

4 Rev. E. L. Cutts, *Scenes and Characters of the Middle Ages*, 191.

echoing the mystery and rhythms of Mother Ocean. Avid shell collector and architect Frank Lloyd Wright based a number of his designs on them, most notably the spiraling Guggenheim Museum in New York City.[5]

Who hasn't succumbed to gathering a few shells when walking along a beach? While their beauty may attract us, their energy has a far greater pull. For this reason, we may find that we are drawn to shells that are not perfectly formed baubles. And, because no two shells are exactly alike, they serve as reminders that we are all unique and beautiful, too.

Some shells come to us as gifts and some as oracular guidance. I often think of the shell that came into my hand as I spoke the Wave Blessing and my double find of the sand dollars. Shells speak to us—so let's learn more about them.

SEASHELLS: AN INTRODUCTION

Seashells can be thought of as the external skeletons of soft-bodied creatures called mollusks. There are five classes of shells, but let's focus on the three major ones, listed here.

- Gastropods—also called univalves—have one shell. Most gastropod shells coil, but some are simply dome- or cone-shaped. They include abalones, conchs (pronounced *kongks*), cowries, moons, limpets, periwinkles, and whelks.

- Bivalves have two shells that are joined by a hinge of ligament and muscle. They include clams, muscles, oysters, and scallops.

- Cephalopods have tentacles and well-developed heads. They include nautilus, squid, octopus, and cuttlefish.

While shells have many detailed parts, let's look at the most important. This brief glossary lists the terms used in this book.

---

5 Marlene Hurley Marshall, *Shell Chic*, 7.

Seashell Anatomy: Some Terms to Know

Aperture: The opening at the front of a gastropod.

Apex: The top or tip of a gastropod shell, where its growth began.

Bivalve: A mollusk with a hinged double shell, such as a clam.

Body whorl: The largest and last-formed section of a shell that contains the soft body of a gastropod.

Byssus: Silky threads used by some mollusks (usually bivalves) to anchor themselves to rocks or other stationary objects.

Columella: The central spiraled pillar of a gastropod shell that can be seen through the aperture.

Distral coil: Clockwise direction of a gastropod's shell coil.

Gastropod: A mollusk with a single shell.

Lip: The edge of a gastropod's aperture, usually composed of inner and outer lips.

Sinistral: Counterclockwise direction of a gastropod's shell coil.

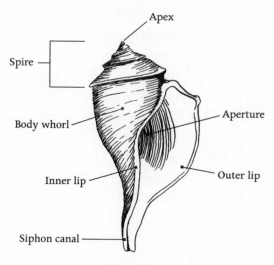

A gastropod shell's basic parts

Siphon canal: A tube for carrying water in and out of a gastropod's body.

Spire: The whorls that rise above the final body whorl.

Whorl: One coil around the axis of a gastropod shell.

Conch or Whelk?

These are the shells we hold to our ear to hear the sound of the ocean. But which are conchs, which are whelks? Not surprisingly, there's much confusion on this point. For one thing, the common name "conch" can refer to either a *Busycon* or a *Strombus* and "whelk" can indicate a *Busycon* or a *Buccinum*. Clear, right? What makes it even more confusing is that the experts don't always agree on the distinctions. I will share with you my humble understanding—but if it differs from yours, stay with what makes most sense to you. Nobody has spoken the last word on this question.

One rule of thumb: a whelk tapers dramatically to a narrow funnel, called a siphon canal, whereas a conch tapers more moderately and "usually has a broad flaring lip."[6] The Florida Horse Conch (*Pleuroploca gigantean*) stands in a complete contradiction to this, but for the most part this distinction holds true. Another difference: whelks tend to be a cold-water species (*Buccinum* family) and conchs are more tropical (*Strombidae* family)—but of course there are exceptions.

Both conchs and whelks are coiled, as are most univalve or single-shelled mollusks. The coil usually spirals in a clockwise direction—regardless of which side of the equator the animal resides on—forming a right-handed or distral coil. One that goes in the opposite direction is called left-handed or sinistrally coiled.[7] To tell the difference, hold the apex (the top of the coil) up with the opening toward you. If the opening is on your right the coil is distral, if it is on your left it is sinistral. In energy work,

6 N. J. and Jacquelyn Berrill, *1001 Questions Answered About the Seashore*, 78.

7 Abbott, *Kingdom of the Seashell*, 36.

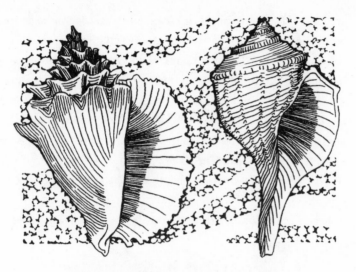

*Comparison of shape: A conch shell (left) generally
tapers more moderately than a whelk (right).*

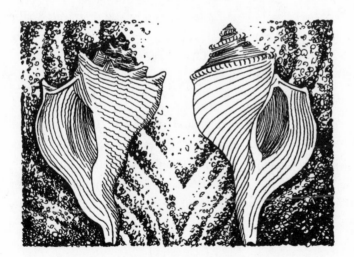

*The whelk on the left has a sinistral (left-handed) coil;
the one on the right has a distral (right-handed) coil.*

the direction of the spiral can be used to emphasize clockwise or counter-clockwise flow, to send energy outward to to pull it in, respectively.

The rare left-handed Indian Chank shell (*Turbinella pyrum*) is sacred to people of the Hindu faith. A one-in-ten-thousand find, it is associated with the god Vishnu and is used in ritual.[8] According to their legends, Vishnu rescued the sacred Hindu scriptures that had been hidden in a left-handed chank at the bottom of the ocean. For this reason, it became a symbol of wisdom,[9] an attribute that has been passed along to the Lightning Whelk (*Busycon contrarium*) because of its similarity to the Chank shell.

Let's get to know some of these exquisite, mysterious creatures.

THE SHELLS

Abalone

There are about 100 species of abalone worldwide, some used medicinally. Abalones belong to the *Haliotidae* family, and their iridescent mother-of-pearl interiors glow like shimmering waves. The interior of the Paua Abalone (*Haliotis iris*) is called "sea opal."[10] The Donkey's Ear (*H. asinine*) species has a more oblong shape. Abalones in general are nicknamed Ear shells and Sea Ears.

Appearance: Abalones are thick and oval or elliptically shaped with a
whorl ridge that is studded with holes for respiration.
Associations: Healing, prosperity; Donkey's Ear: foolishness.
Uses: These shells are frequently used as smudge bowls for cleansing
the energy of an area. Abalone's beautiful interior energetically attracts abundance.

---

8 Abbott, *Shells*, 10.

9 Michelle Hanson, *Ocean Oracle*, 60.

10 Ibid., 58.

Angel Wing

These shells belong to the *Pholadidae* family. If you find both halves of an Angel Wing (*Cyrtopleura costata*) shell, you will see how they got their name: when opened flat they resemble a pair of angel's wings. The False Angel Wing (*Petricola pholadiformis*) and Wing shell (*Pholas campechiensis*) are similar to the Angel Wing. Despite their delicate appearance, they can bore into clay, wood, and some types of rock.

Appearance: Angel Wings are elongated and delicate, with ribs that run from the hinge to the outer edges, suggesting feathers.

Associations: Determination, freedom.

Uses: This shell helps raise our spirits and lets our intentions soar. They can also aid in contact with angelic energy.

Ark

Shells in the *Arcidae* family are strongly ribbed and usually attach themselves to rocks with a threadlike anchor called a byssus. The Blood Ark (*Anadara ovalis*) is so called because it is the only bivalve with red blood.[11] The Incongruous Ark (*A. brasiliana*) is aptly named because one of its two shells is larger than the other.

Appearance: Arks are sturdy and broad. Most are somewhat rectangular but some are more oval. All have radial ribs.

Associations: Safety, shelter.

Uses: Arks help us move inward for reflection. They also aid in finding stability in the outer world.

---

11 Kenneth Gosner, *A Field Guide to the Atlantic Seashore*, 146.

Auger

The *Terebridae* family has about 300 species, including the Common American Auger (*Terebra dislocata*) and the Marlinspike Auger (*T. maculata*). These animals move below the surface of the sand, leaving a noticeable trail. The auger's energy is focused and can be instrumental in projecting intention.

Appearance: Augers are elongated and slender with pointed spires that can be smooth or sculpted. These tiny lances have a wide range of colorful patterns.

Associations: Focus, protection.

Uses: They help us project and send energy.

Bear's Paw

This clam (*Hippopus hippopus*) is from the family of Giant Clams, *Tridacnidae*. Also known as the Horse's Hoof clam, it usually lives near coral formations. These shells were popular in the late nineteenth century and were commonly found in Victorian drawing rooms.

Appearance: The Bear's Paw clam is thick and heavy with wide ribbing and scalloped edges.

Associations: Power, strength, vitality.

Uses: The energy of this shell is balanced between male and female. While it exudes the qualities mentioned above, it also offers nurturing, protection, and warmth.

Carrier

These shells belong to the *Xenophoridae* family. A carrier uses empty shells of other mollusks and miscellaneous debris for portable camouflage by cementing them to its own shell. The Latin name *Xenophora* means "bearer of foreigners."[12] Examples include the Pallid Carrier (*Xenophora pallidula*) of Japan, the Atlantic Carrier (*X. conchyliophora*), and the Curly Carrier (*X. crispa*).

---

12 Abbott, *Kingdom of the Seashell*, 96.

Appearance: A carrier looks like a moving pile of shells.

Associations: Timid, wanting to hide, clinging or trouble with bonds, greed.

Uses: Carriers can help us come out of our own shell, get over shyness, and deal with greedy people; they also aid in breaking away from clinging people.

Clam

Clams encompass a wide range of species in several families: Hard-Shelled clams or *Mercenaria mercenaria* (think clam chowder), Soft-Shelled clams or *Mya arenaria* (also known as steamers), and Surf clams or *Spisula solidissima*, to name a few. Some clams are very colorful and some are almost wing-shaped, earning them the nickname Butterfly shells (those of the *Tellinidae* family). Others twist around on themselves, giving the shell the look of a ram's horn (family *Glossidae*). The Chocolate-Flamed Venus clam (*Lioconcha castrensis*) has dark brown zigzag lines that can resemble ancient writing.

Appearance: Clams can be circular, oval, or triangular. Their colors range from white to dark brown. Some have a papery coating over the exterior of the shell.

Associations: Abundance, communication, foundation, groundedness, healing energy, love, purification, stability, vitality.

Uses: Clams can help us find our place in the world, hold a confidence, and protect our emotions.

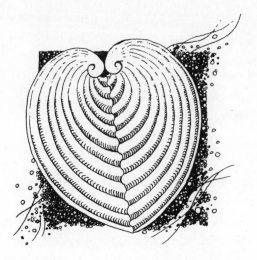

A cockle shell is heart-shaped when viewed from the side.

Cockle

Members of the *Cardiidae* family, there are over 200 species of cockles worldwide.[13] These shells have been used for food, ornamentation, and currency as far back as 3000 BCE in Mesopotamia.[14] Prehistoric graves in Lincolnshire, England, were discovered to be filled with cockle shells, suggesting that they were a symbol of death and rebirth.[15] Cockles are also called Heart Clams because when viewed from the side with both shells intact, they appear heart-shaped.[16] Additionally, they were used in ancient medicine because they were believed to be good for the heart.

Appearance: Cockles are heavily ribbed and can be round or oval.

Associations: Balance, contentment (as in "warm the cockles of the heart"), dawn, gateway to a new life, love.

Uses: Cockles are very good for centering and calming personal energy. They also represent new beginnings.

13 Fred Woodward, *Identifying Shells*, 69.

14 Jackie Leatherbury Douglass and Roger Tory Peterson, *Peterson First Guide to Shells of North America*, 86.

15 Harold Bayley, *Archaic England*, 248.

16 Abbott, *Shells*, 56.

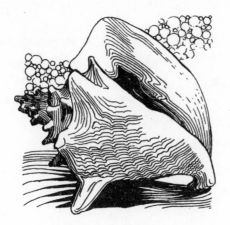

The Queen Conch

Conch

Shells of the *Strombidae* family are called true conchs. With the tip of the apex removed, this shell is blown like a trumpet in India and Sri Lanka to "open the heavens" for ritual.[17] In Hawaii, the conch is sounded to call spirits or to cleanse the energy of a space. The Pink Conch, also known as the Queen Conch (*Strombus gigas*), occasionally produces pink pearls.

Appearance: Conchs have a spiraling shape, usually with a broad flaring lip. True conchs are distinguished by a notch in the outer lip at the front (lower/smaller) end.

Associations: Knowledge, love magic, speech, sacredness, vitality, wisdom; the deities Devi, Vishnu, and Yemanja.

Uses: Conchs are great for clearing negative energy and preparing an area for an event or activity. Their energy can aid in our moving inward for reflection.

---

17 Daya Sarai Chocron, *The Healing Power of Seashells*, 34.

Cone

Worldwide, there are over 300 species of cones—members of the family *Conidae*. These shells have a highly developed poison for killing prey, and the Geography Cone (*Conus geographys*) has even caused human deaths.[18] Even so, they are among the most widely collected shells because of their remarkably beautiful colors and intricate patterns. Only a few types of cones spiral sinistrally.

Appearance: Cone shells are, well, cone-shaped with generally (but not always) flattened spires and elongated openings. They come in a stunning range of patterns.

Associations: Impatience, perfection, potential danger, recognition.

Uses: Cones can boost our protective energy as well as support our transformation as we progress through life.

Cowry

Belonging to the *Cypraeidae* family, cowries number more than 200 species worldwide.[19] A wide range of cultures have used them for secular and sacred purposes. In relation to the Great Mother Goddess, cowries can represent both vulva and pregnant belly, symbolizing abundance, fertility and (pro)creative powers. The Hindu goddess Hayagriva is usually depicted rising from a yoni-symbol cowry-like shell. The ancient Romans associated cowries with the goddess Venus and gave them as gifts to brides.[20] The cowry's long aperture has also been likened to a mouth— and even seen as the mouthpiece of the gods. Oshun (a goddess of fresh water) taught the Yoruba people of Nigeria how to use the shells for divination (see pages 67–76).[21]

The Money Cowry (*Cypraea moneta*) and the Gold Ring (*C. annulus*) were used as currency in Asia, Africa, and Malaysia. The first coins made

---

18 Bruno Sabelli, *Simon & Schuster's Guide to Shells*, 236.

19 Woodward, *Identifying Shells*, 29.

20 Daya Sarai Chocron, *The Healing Power of Seashells*, 31.

21 Clare Gibson, *Goddess Symbols*, 76.

*The cowry has a serrated opening on one side
and a rounded belly on the other.*

of metal in China (circa 600 BCE) were cast in the shape of cowry shells.[22] The Romans called cowry shells *porci* or *porculi*, "little pigs."[23] In the ancient world, the pig was a symbol of fecundity and prosperity, associated with powerful goddesses such as the Greek Demeter, whose sacred rituals included the sacrifice of pigs.[24] Combining the symbolism of vulva and sow, the Greek word *choiros* means both pig and female genitals,[25] and may be mistaken for the root of the word cowry. The English word *cowry* is derived from the Hindi *kauri*.[26]

Appearance: Cowries are small and roughly egg-shaped. They have a rounded side and a flat underside whose opening is a long serrated slit. The finish is glossy and enamel-like.

Associations: Abundance, fertility, growth, groundedness, oracles, prosperity.

Uses: Cowries are excellent for divination, manifesting our intentions, and soul work.

---

22 Woodward, *Identifying Shells*, 6.

23 Abbott, *Kingdom of the Seashell*, 178.

24 Diana Ferguson, *The Magickal Year*, 65.

25 Philip Herbst, *Wimmin Wimps & Wallflowers*, 226.

26 Walter Skeat, *The Concise Dictionary of English Etymology*, 98.

Crown

Actually a type of whelk, the Crown Conch (*Melongena corona*) belongs to the *Melongenidae* family.

Appearance: Projections on top of the body whorl make it resemble a crown. These shells vary widely in color and stripe patterns.
Associations: Crown chakra, connection with the divine.
Uses: Crowns help uplift energy, boost intention, and aid in meditation.

Drupe

Members of the family *Thaididae*, drupes are cousins to the murex. They are usually small and unassuming but have beautifully colored apertures. Drupes are widespread in the Indo-Pacific region; the Purple Drupe (*Drupa morum*) is one of the most common.

Appearance: Drupes are small, thick knobby shells with flattish spires. They have varied and colorful apertures.
Associations: Reflection, self-assurance.
Uses: Drupes help us discover and grow comfortable with who we are.

Frog

To picture this member of the *Bursidae* family, think of a squat (froglike) triton shell (see pages 106–107). It looks very similar, but can be distinguished by a groove in the upper corner of the aperture. Examples include the Common Frog (*Bursa rana*), Noble Frog (*B. margaritula*), and Japanese Frog (*B. dunkeri*).

Appearance: Yellowish to brown, frog shells are solid and thick with angular whorls. Their round apertures have a distinctive groove.
Association: Momentum.
Uses: Frog shells can help us mobilize a situation and shake things up.

Helmet

Members of the *Cassidae* family, these medium- to large-sized "Bonnet shells" are frequently mistaken for conchs. Of about eighty helmet species, the King Helmet (*Cassis tuberoa*) is the largest example, and the best known. It is used for carved cameo jewelry, as is the Black Helmet (*C. madagascariensis*), also known as the Queen Helmet.[27]

Appearance: These shells are heavy with short spires and wide whorls.
   Their long apertures have a thick-toothed outer lip. The general
   shape suggests an ancient army helmet.
Associations: Groundedness, protection, strength.
Uses: Helmets can aid in sea centerings to keep us grounded. They can
   also be used to honor an ally.

Janthina

These shells belong to the family *Janthinidae*. Also called Purple Snails, Janthina Snails (*Janthina janthina*), spend their lives on the open ocean. Common in the Sargasso Sea, they stay afloat on a raft of frothy bubbles that they create.[28] The Mediterranean Purple Sea Snail (*J. nitens*) is more fragile than its Atlantic cousin.

Appearance: Low, rounded spires and almost flat whorls make these
   shells look like inverted tops.
Associations: Faith, peace, trust.
Uses: Janthinas help us build our intuition and develop trust that the
   universe will provide abundance. They show us how to be at peace
   with ourselves and, when necessary, to simply go with the flow of
   life.

---

27 Abbott, *Kingdom of the Seashell*, 230.
28 Ibid., 57.

Jingle

These bivalves of the *Anomiidae* family are almost as common as sand along America's Atlantic beaches. Jingle Shells (*Anomia simplex*) are rarely found intact, but the halves look different. The right side (lower valve) has a circular hole near the hinge through which the animal anchors itself to a rock or other surface. This half is rarely found.[29]

Appearance: Jingles are irregularly shaped circles or ovals, very light, translucent and fragile. Their iridescent sheen ranges in color from white or yellow to black or red.

Associations: The ephemeral realm, trust.

Uses: Jingles help us learn to trust our intuition and judge when it is wise to let go and ride with the tides of life.

Limpet

Limpets are found throughout the world. Resembling little hats, they have an interior that often looks like porcelain, sometimes brightly colored. The Giant Owl Limpet (*Lottia gigantea*) is so named because its interior has an owl-like pattern. True limpets belong to the *Acmaidae* and *Lottiidae* families. Keyhole Limpets are members of the *Fissurellidae* family and are so named because of the hole at the apex of their shells.

Appearance: Limpets are oval or irregularly shaped and slightly conical. They have a wide range of colors and patterns.

Associations: Confidence, courage, the ability to nurture, strength, tenaciousness, wisdom.

Uses: Limpets remind us of the value of introspection and self-development.

---

29 Abbott and Morris, *Shells of the Atlantic*, 38.

The cone-shaped limpet shell resembles a little hat.

Lion's Paw

A member of the *Pectinidae* family of scallop shells, the Lion's Paw (*Lyropecten nodosa,* also classified as *Nodipecten nodesus*) is sought after by collectors.[30] It is shaped like other scallops with the addition of "knuckles"— enlarged hollow areas that the animal can fill with fluid.

Appearance: Lion's Paws are robust, heavy shells with broad folds. They
 range in color from reddish brown to bright orange.
Associations: Protection, strength.
Uses: Lion's Paws help us build inner strength and confidence.

Miter

Named for their resemblance to bishop's headgear, these shells belong to the *Mitrinae* family. Examples include the Episcopal Miter (*Mitra mitra*) and Cardinal Miter (*M. cardinalis*). Several hundred species can be found throughout the world, mainly in warm, temperate locations.

Appearance: Miters are somewhat elongated and conical, with a smooth
 or spirally sculpted texture and a tall, pointed spire. Most are
 brightly colored.

---

30 Ibid., 29.

Associations: Peace, spirituality.

Uses: Because of their association with clergy, these shells calm our
energy and help with spiritual introspection.

Moon

Found throughout the world, these members of the *Naticidae* family are
also called Necklace Shells.[31] The Atlantic Moon *(Polinices duplicatus)* has
the common name of Shark's Eye. Moon shells were used as talismans in
some Celtic burials, sometimes scattered over the body, sometimes below
it. They were also symbolically placed near the hands and feet or in a pattern above the head.[32]

Moon shells embody two powerful symbols: the circle and the spiral.
With no beginning or end, the circle represents the eternal cycles of the
natural world. The spiral, a symbol of vitality and of the Great Mother
Goddess, is a dynamic expression of energy that moves both inward and
outward. It represents the future as well as the past.

Appearance: Moon shells are round and tightly coiled, with a short or
flat spire. Their colors and patterns vary widely.

Associations: Cycles, clarity, the Great Mother Goddess, harmony, life,
non-judgment, protection, rebirth, self-sufficiency.

Uses: Moons can teach us to roll with life's turbulence and to move inward without losing sight of what's around us. They can also help us
find answers to questions that are important to us.

Murex

Worldwide, more than a thousand species of murex can be found—also
known as Rock Shells, of the *Muricidae* family. These shells were the source
of the rosy-purple dye that became known as royal tyrian purple. Highly
valued by the ancient Phoenicians and Romans, the dye was later used by
the Roman Catholic and Episcopal churches to color bishops' robes.[33] The

---

31 Woodward, *Identifying Shells*, 32.

32 Jan Fries, *Cauldron of the Gods*, 52.

33 Abbott, *Kingdom of the Seashell*, 154.

The moon shell symbolizes the power of the circle and the spiral.

Venus Comb Murex (*Murex pectin*), with its long thin spines, is one of the most striking examples.

Appearance: Murex shells range from heavy to delicate, with whorls that are smooth, spiny, or nodular. Colors and patterns also vary widely.

Associations: Intensity, protection, reaching out.

Uses: The murex can help us summon courage to overcome adversity.

Mussel

Known to seafood lovers everywhere, the Blue Mussel (*Mytilus edulis*) and its Mediterranean cousin (*M. galloprovincialis*) belong to the *Mytilidae* family. The larger brown variety is known as the Horse Mussel (*Modiolus modiolus*). Mussels are usually found attached to rocks and piers or in the mud and sand of shallow water.

Appearance: Mussels are elongated, pear-shaped shells, ranging in color from purple-black to blue or brown. The interior is pearly.

Associations: Life-giving, stability, community, the moon.

Uses: Mussels help us see that we can weather life's storms.

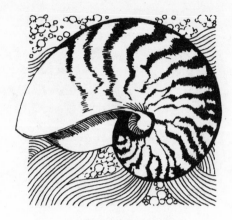

The Chambered Nautilus

Nautilus

The only cephalopod that produces a shell, the Chambered Nautilus (*Nautilus pompilius*) belongs to the *Nautilidae* family. It is so named because the shell consists of separate chambers that are created as the animal grows. Its geometry is one of nature's examples of mathematical perfection, inspiring the discovery of Fibonacci's of Golden Ratio. The Chambered Nautilus generally lives some two hundred feet deep in the ocean. It is nearly the last of its class of cephalopods that were abundant 400 million years ago.[34] Like the Moon Shell, the Nautilus embodies the symbols of the circle and the spiral.

The Paper Nautilus (*Argonauta argo*) is not a true seashell (external skeletal protection), but a receptacle to protect the animal's eggs.[35]

Appearance: The Nautilus has a creamy white shell with broad, wavy brown stripes. The interior is pearly iridescent.
Associations: Ancestors, balance, endings/beginnings.
Uses: The Nautilus can help us find our place in the world, acknowledge change and seek balance in all things.

---

34 Ibid., 19.

35 Woodward, *Identifying Shells*, 77.

Olive

The glossy exterior of this shell, a member of the *Olividae* family, made it popular for use in jewelry by Indo-Pacific islanders.[36] Examples include the Carnelian Olive (*Oliva carneola*), the Common Olive (*O. oliva*), and the Tent Olive (*O. porphyria*).

Appearance: Olives are smooth and cylindrical. An elongated aperture has a distinct posterior siphonal notch.

Associations: Abundance, opportunity.

Uses: These shells help us reflect on the simple gifts in life.

Oyster

A food source since prehistoric times,[37] true oysters belong to the *Ostreidae* family. Examples include the Common European (*Ostrea edulis*) and Crested (*O. equestris*). The ancient Greeks believed that dew or rain taken in by the oyster would ripen into a pearl.[38] (In fact, pearls are formed around grains of sand or any other irritant.) Oysters of various families—as well as some other types of shells—also produce pearls. Wing Oysters (*Pincyada imbricata*) and Pearl Oysters (*Pteria hirundo*) are members of the *Pteriidae* family.

Appearance: Oysters are irregular, rounded, or elongated in shape and have a variety of colors.

Associations: Fertility, hidden beauty, love, treasure, vitality, the moon.

Uses: As symbols of good luck, oysters can help us attract prosperity as well as a lover.

---

36 Ibid., 51.

37 Ibid., 63.

38 Bassett, *Legends and Superstitions*, 264.

Periwinkle

Fifty to 100 species of these shore-dwelling snails, of the family *Littorini-dae*, are found throughout the world. The smallest is the Rough Periwin-kle (*Littorina saxatilis*). Next in size are the Northern Yellow or Smooth Periwinkle (*L. obtusata*) and the Common Periwinkle (*L. littorea*), respec-tively. Usually found clinging to rocks in tidal pools, periwinkles are in "mid-passage" evolving from marine animal to land dweller.[39]

Appearance: Periwinkles are solid little shells with short spires and cir-cular apertures. Colors range widely. Smooth Periwinkles are bright yellow or orange with virtually no spire.

Associations: Friendship, groundedness, integrity.

Uses: These shells can help us hold focus and stay centered.

Sand Dollar

I include the sand dollar here although it is not a seashell, but a type of sea urchin related to the starfish.[40] The sand dollar moves between the worlds of water and earth, burying itself in the sand and soft mud on the ocean floor. The Common Sand Dollar (*Echinarachnius parma*) and the Keyhole Urchin (*Mellita testudinata*) are easily recognized by the five-petaled shape etched in their center. The sand dollar has been associated with the life of Jesus, its five-pointed pattern representing both the star of Bethlehem and the five wounds inflicted at the crucifixion.[41]

Appearance: Sand dollars are irregularly shaped, round and flat with a five-pointed flowerlike pattern and five holes. The color is usually white or tan.

Associations: Awareness, balance, divine energy, hidden meaning, transformation, wisdom.

Uses: Sand dollars help us seek wholeness and acquire knowledge. They are an aid in keeping confidences and protecting emotions.

---

39 Carson, *Edge of the Sea*, 50.

40 Ibid., 264.

41 Michelle Hanson, *Ocean Oracle*, 70.

The sand dollar has a five-petaled design.

Scallop

Not only were Aphrodite and Venus depicted arising fully formed on scallop shells, so too were a number of Aztec and Mayan goddesses. Throughout ancient Europe, the scallop shell was used "as a symbol of religion, mysticism, and of sex."[42] Of the *Pectinidae* family, more than 400 species are found worldwide.

As a design motif, the scallop has been used in personal ornamentation, fabric and furniture décor, and architecture. In the early years of the Christian church it was a badge of pilgrimage. On heraldic banners, a scallop with two slits (or "eyes" as they were called) indicated that a knight had been in battle and had searched for the Holy Grail.[43] The energy of a scallop is radiant and healing.

Appearance: Scallops are fan-shaped and somewhat flat. Of the true
   scallops (*Pectin* family), one shell or valve is more concave than the
   other. Their colors range from white to a variety of brilliant hues.
Associations: Beauty, birth, change, fertility, harmony, healing, journey/
   travel, regeneration, relaxation, spirituality, the moon.

---

42 Abbott, *Kingdom of the Seashell*, 188–189.
43 Ibid., 194.

Uses: As a symbol of pilgrimage, scallops aid in spiritual rejuvenation.
They are instrumental in removing energy blocks and keeping us
centered. With them we can search the depths of our souls. They
help us know that we are all beautiful.

Slipper

From above, slipper shells appear as rounded little mounds; underneath
is a protective shelf that covers part of the animal's body and gives the
shell a moccasin-like appearance. When I was a child I thought of them as
rowboats for fairies. Slippers live in colonies attached to rocks and each
other. They can change sex (from male to female) as necessity dictates.[44]
These shells belong to the *Crepidulidae* family.

Appearance: The flattened oval shell has an interior "shelf" that forms a
slipperlike shape. Color is cream, yellow, brown or reddish brown.
Associations: Balance, community, generosity, nonconformity,
transformation.
Uses: Slippers aid in weathering transitions, and they support us as we
help others.

Spider

This type of conch with a spiderlike appearance has nine known species,
with the Common Spider *(Lambis lambis)* being the most widely found.
The *Lambis Scorpius* resembles a scorpion.

Appearance: The spider conch has "fingers"—up to six inches long—
that extend from the shell's flaring lip.
Associations: Maturity, responsibility, self-defense.
Uses: Spider shells help us learn how to stand our ground.

---

44 Ibid., 29.

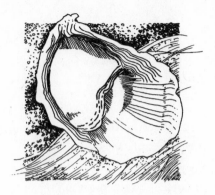

The slipper shell's interior

Spindle

These members of the *Fasciolariidae* family are so named because they resemble yarn spindles; they are also called Tulip shells. They include the
Wavy-Edge Spindle (*Fusinus undatus*) and Long-Tailed Spindle (*F. longi-
caudatis*). The animal buries itself in the sand or mud, using its long siphon canal as a snorkel to suck seawater into its gills. The Shinbone Tibia
(*Tibia fusus fusus*), also called the Spindle Tibia, is exceptionally long and
thin. It belongs to the *Strombidae* (conch) family.

Appearance: Spindle shells have a high spire, many elongated whorls,
   and a long, straight canal. They range from white to multi-colored.
Associations: Relationships, the goddess Freya.
Uses: These shells help us learn to "spin" or create our own path in life.

Sundial

These shells belong to the *Architectonicidae* family. The Common Sundial
(*Architectonica nobilis*) and the Giant Sundial (*A. maxima*) are examples
of this small group of disk-like shells.

Appearance: Sundials are round with a stubby apex.
Associations: Cycles, movement, patience.
Uses: These shells can help us get out of linear ruts and move on.

Thorny Oyster

From the *Spondylidae* family, these "oysters" are cousins to the scallops. Examples include the American Thorny Oyster (*Spondylus americanus*) and Pacific Thorny Oyster (*S. princeps*). They are also called Chrysanthemum shells.

Appearance: Elongated spines protrude at various angles. These shells vary greatly in size and can be very colorful.
Associations: Creativity, defense.
Uses: Thorny oysters can help us reach out to project energy or intention.

Top Shell

Found worldwide, there are hundreds of members of the *Trochidae* family, which has a number of genuses. The West Indian Top Snail (*Cittarium pica*) is frequently an ingredient in Caribbean chowders.[45]

Appearance: Top shells have a conical spiral and a pyramidal shape. Colors and patterns vary widely.
Associations: Dynamic energy of the circle and spiral; pyramid power.
Uses: Top shells aid us in centering; they also help get energy flowing.

Triton

These rugged yet decorative shells, related to the murex, are of the *Ranellidae* family. With a hole drilled into the apex they can be used as horns. Triton's Trumpet (*Charonia tritonis*) is the largest and best known because it is used to call people to worship.[46] It is also called the Pacific Trumpet Triton; there is also an Atlantic Trumpet Triton (*C. variegata*). In Greek legend, Poseidon called his son Triton to blow this trumpet and subdue floods. This scene was depicted on a Roman coin in 400 BCE.[47]

---

45 Eugene Kaplen, *A Field Guide to Southeastern and Caribbean Seashores*, 108.

46 Woodward, *Identifying Shells*, 7.

47 Abbott, *Shells*, 10.

Appearance: Tritons are solid and sculpted with strong riblike areas. The thick outer lip is often toothed. These shells have a wide range of colors and patterns.

Associations: Community, joy, the element air.

Uses: With tritons we can send out intentions and prayers.

Turkey Wing

A type of ark shell, the Turkey Wing (*Arca zebra*) is a member of the *Arcidae* family. In Bermuda, this ark is baked into pies.[48]

Appearance: These shells are elongated, wing-shaped and yellowish-white in color with red-brown striping.

Associations: Freedom.

Uses: These shells help us lift moods and shift emotions.

Whelk

About 800 species of whelk can be found worldwide. The Lightning Whelk (*Busycon contrarium*) is one of the few shells with a left-handed coil. For this reason, it is commonly mistaken for the sacred Indian Chank shell, mentioned earlier, or simply employed as a substitute—adding to the confusion over these seashells. The core or *columellae* of whelks were strung together and used as money by Native Americans. White wampum beads were also made from whelks.

Appearance: Whelks are globular-shaped near the apex with a long, tapering siphon. They have a wide range of colors and sizes.

Associations: Dramatic life changes, good fortune, imagination, inspiration, wisdom.

Uses: Whelks help us find guidance, especially for spiritual development.

---

48 Abbott and Morris, *Shells of the Atlantic*, 8.

Journal Questions

1. Why do you think people are fascinated with seashells?

2. What is your experience when meditating with a shell?

3. If there is a particular type of shell that attracts you, what is it? Why might that be?

4. Can you visualize a walk along a beach collecting as many shells as you can carry? How would that feel?

V

SEA FETCHES, TOTEM ANIMALS, AND MYTHICAL SEA CREATURES

*W*hat happens in actual experience is that while people are often expecting little butterfly people, or perhaps the Lordly Ones of the high faery tradition . . . they meet something quite different.

R. J. STEWART
The Living World of Faery

SINCE THE DAWN OF HUMANITY, people have sought ways to communicate with beings of the spirit realm. Whether we call these entities angels, spirit guides, faeries, or ancestors, many of the human techniques for contacting them are remarkably similar. In the words of Dr. Wayne Dyer, "Spirit eludes our attempts to explain and define it because it's a dimension beyond beginnings and ends, beyond boundaries, beyond symbols and beyond form itself."[1]

If you have ever felt aided by unseen hands, you may already believe in the Otherworld of spirit—or you may be skeptical and question your own sanity. I have felt this type of aid, and although I doubt my perceptions at times, my personal experiences and intuition have led me to acknowledge the reality of this spirit world. Still, I believe that a certain amount of skepticism is healthy. Whenever I am not sure an experience is "real," I ask that a sign be presented within my everyday life to confirm it.

FINDING YOUR SEA FETCH

When seeking a spirit guide, we don't have to look to mythical creatures to find a range of marvelous (and sometimes mysterious) sea animals. (We will, however, visit some mythical creatures and beings later in this section.) Some of our potential guides or totem animals for Sea Magic live entirely in the sea, some split their time between earthly and watery worlds, and still others take to the skies—and yet the sea is their home.

---

1 Dyer, *Power of Intention*, 22.

Let us turn to these creatures to find our sea fetch. Known variously as animal allies, totems, helpers, spirit guides, and fetches, they are common to Native American, Celtic, and other cultures where shamanistic practices flourished. I prefer the term *fetch* because it indicates an ally that brings you to knowledge. It happens that the word *fetch* also refers to the distance that a wave runs across the ocean.[2] As a result, the sea fetch is a bringer of wisdom from Mother Ocean.

Animals can act as messengers as well as sources of inspiration, healing, and guidance. Those associated with the sea are generally considered wise and powerful. A totem animal or sea fetch can remain with you for your entire life, or it may come briefly into your life to guide you through a particular phase or turning point. Some are merely messengers that have one brief communication or idea to relay. You may also encounter one that may be difficult to deal with at first. This type of fetch usually appears to draw out a side of you that has been ignored. At first this fetch may seem fearsome or contrary, but in the long run what it helps bring to your surface level of consciousness can be very important. According to Caitlin Matthews, "the appearance of talking beasts in folk story denotes a shift of emphasis to a deeper level of awareness; such beasts are not anthropomorphic animals, but archetypal forms."[3]

Animals that present themselves to you may symbolize who you are, or they may possess qualities that you would like to express in your life. Let's take a brief overview of qualities associated with several potential sea fetches. We'll look at them in more detail over the following pages.

Twelve Sea Fetches and Their Associated Qualities

Albatross: Solitude, survival, the ability to wonder.

Crab: Adaptability, clarity of vision, creativity, growth, renewal, rebirth.

Dolphin: Communication, community, intuition, joy, serenity, strength.

---

2 Carson, *Sea Around Us*, 92.

3 Caitlin Matthews, *Mabon and the Guardians of Celtic Britain*, 156.

Manatee: Gentleness, ability to nurture, relaxation.

Otter: Companionship, duty, friendship, loyalty, transformation.

Penguin: Balance, independence, inner strength, wisdom.

Polar Bear: Ability to nurture, protection, power, spiritual guidance, strength.

Salmon: Cycles, determination, healer, progress.

Sea Gull: Communication, freedom, responsibility, simplicity.

Seal: Balance, creativity, curiosity, playfulness.

Turtle: Fertility, immortality, longevity, opportunity, perseverance.

Whale: Communication, community, creativity, cycles, harmony.

Some of the animals' qualities, such as the crab's, may surprise you. However, the crab is associated with health and vision (mental and psychic), and its energy is useful for protection from negativity. Perhaps the inclusion of the polar bear surprised you, too. While all of its relatives are clearly earthbound creatures, the polar bear is also known as the water bear and the ice bear. It is very much at home in the waters of the North Atlantic and Arctic Oceans.

A fetch can make itself known in various ways. In fact, its image may continually appear to you until you realize and acknowledge it. Thereafter, an appearance may indicate a need for contact or reassurance—or it may be a signal that only you and your fetch will understand.

One way that birds communicate their presence and intent is through the gifting of a feather. I have been drawn to seagulls since I was a child and I have felt comforted by their calls. When I moved into my house in Maine and stepped out onto the back porch for the first time, I was greeted with the cry of gulls and a snowy white feather on my steps. I felt that I had truly come home.

Still, as with the "signs" communicated by seashells, I believe that a touch of skepticism is healthy. The difference between a message and an ordinary experience is the timing and the undeniable feeling that it holds meaning. Keep your senses open, ask questions of yourself and the fetch, then trust your intuition. If you are still unsure, ask for further signs. If a fetch was communicating with you, you will receive them.

The sea journey presented here will help you find your sea fetch. Of course, there is the possibility that a mythical creature may present itself to you. Don't reject it out of hand. Go with the flow if your intuition tells you that there is something to be learned. Examine why you might be drawn to it and then research as much as you can about it. Our feelings and inner experiences are valid and do not require a stamp of approval from other people. Stay truthful to yourself.

TWELVE FETCHES IN DETAIL

Let's look at these fetches more closely. But remember, this is by no means a complete list of potential candidates. Any animal connected with the ocean can act as your sea fetch. Sea birds—see the albatross and sea gull— have a special spiritual energy that crosses the realms of heaven, sea, and land, energetically linking the three permanent elements of air, water, and earth. But every creature has its own totemic power. Which one speaks to you?

Albatross

This rare oceanic wanderer can show us the ethereal realms beyond this world—and within our hearts. At one time the albatross was seen as the "restless spirits of drowned sailors" because of its cry and its endless soaring.[4] With a wingspan greater than other sea birds', albatross can shepherd us on our journey and steer us in the direction we are meant to travel. Albatross teaches us the value of nurturing—even the male sits on the nest—as well as the skills to survive any turbulence we may encounter. With albatross as a guide we can learn to see the magnificence in the world around us and the worlds within us.

Associations: Solitude, survival, the ability to wonder.

---

4 Horace Beck, *Folklore and the Sea*, 291.

Crab

The crab may seem an unlikely guide; however, it has a place in legend and is associated with magical powers. Crabs are found in all oceans. They shed their shells as they grow, which symbolizes renewal and rebirth. As a result, crab can instruct us not to be afraid to change and grow. Crab is adaptable and sensitive, with a clarity of vision that can teach us to keep an eye on our goals and unfold to our own potential. Although crab is shy by nature and stays near shore, we can learn how to come out of our shell and explore the spiritual depths that await our discovery. Crabs may walk sideways—but from this we can learn how to sidestep trouble when necessary yet still meet important issues head-on. As a zodiacal sign, crab is associated with the moon and brings creative energies into play as a spirit guide.

Associations: Adaptability, clarity of vision, creativity, growth, renewal, rebirth.

Crab

Dolphin

The dolphin is an ancient symbol of love goddesses: its name comes from the Greek *delphinos,* meaning "womb."[5] The Celts believed that dolphins carried departed souls to the Isle of the Blessed. To early Christians the dolphin symbolized the resurrection and salvation of Christ. Fond of people and music, dolphin helps us value communication, community, and play. Strength, joy, and serenity are qualities that dolphin can help us cultivate. Ancient mariners believed that dolphins could warn them about approaching storms. Their oracular ability can help us find the way to our individual enlightenment. Dolphin offers support in finding our unique path through life.

Associations: Communication, community, intuition, joy, serenity, strength.

Manatee

In 1493 Christopher Columbus noted in his logbook that his ship encountered sea maidens, which contributed to the scientific order's name of *Sirenia.* Today, our best guess is that Columbus and his crew had spotted manatees.[6] These graceful, slow-moving swimmers have a gentle demeanor and a great deal to teach us. Manatee is shy but curious, teaching us the importance of remaining open to experiences even if they seem frightening. A strong bond develops between a mother manatee and her calf, teaching us that nurturing and gentleness are of utmost importance in relationships. Manatee's lovely, relaxed pace beckons us to take our time and slow down. In rushing, we miss so much of the flavor of life.

Associations: Gentleness, ability to nurture, relaxation.

---

5 Sally Morningstar, *Love Magic,* 31.

6 Dave Taylor, *Florida Manatees,* 47.

Otter

The Celtic people believed otters to be magical animals because they inhabit the netherworld where land meets sea. In legends, otters were shown to be helpful to travelers. The Celts called them "water dogs"[7] because of their appearance as well as their speed and skill. Otter symbolizes companionship and encouragement. Such traits make otter a wise and dutiful guide. As legend suggests, with loyalty, friendship, and playfulness, otter guides us on a quest where the unexpected can occur and deep transformation begins. Associated with the sea god Manannan, otter knows how to keep confidences in order to serve. Otter brings brightness and joy into our world and shows us how to find it on our own.

Associations: Companionship, duty, friendship, loyalty, transformation.

Penguin

Portrayed as a little tuxedoed comic, penguin is anything but this inaccurate caricature. Penguin teaches us that we cannot make quick judgments about people because things are not always what they seem. Penguin gives us an example of how we can be true to ourselves and march to our own rhythm. As fathers, male penguins usually share in the egg incubation process and nursery duties, reminding us that males can be as nurturing as females and also serving as a model of balanced energy. Able to hunker down and weather the harsh Antarctic winter, penguin also teaches us about strength and survival. Emperor penguins in particular spend a lot of time in winter twilight; thus they are familiar with that Otherworldly betwixt-and-between state. With the moon providing the brightest light for several months, penguin gains the wisdom of Luna and passes it to those under its guidance.

Associations: Balance, independence, inner strength, wisdom.

---

7 Anna Franklin, *The Celtic Animal Oracle*, 46.

Penguin

Polar Bear

In general, bears are earthy and grounded, but then there's the polar bear. These indefatigable swimmers, whose massive paws serve as paddles, are equally at home in the water and on land. It has been said that polar bears "could be considered the link between sea and land in the Arctic."[8] Polar bear is a solitary wanderer, spending much of the year on pack ice, going where the floe takes it. As a nomadic wanderer, polar bear is an excellent guide for inner journeys. Strength and protection (especially in Otherworld realms) are hallmarks of polar bear's mystical and spiritual significance. Polar bear has also mastered the art of survival in the physical realm, demonstrating the power of selfless nurturing better than anyone. All who travel are guided by polar bear through the constellation of Ursa Major—the great bear. Polaris, the North Star, the final star in her tail, was used for navigation by sailors for centuries. But polar bear has a playful side, too: the ethereal spirited movement of the Aurora Borealis is

---

8 Richard Perry, *The Polar Worlds*, 193.

also called the "dance of the bears."[9] While polar bear teaches us the joy of dance and play, her semi-hibernation habits also show us the importance of stillness: self-work begins in active stillness.

Associations: Ability to nurture, protection, power, spiritual guidance, strength.

Salmon

Celtic people considered the salmon the oldest and wisest of all creatures. In some legends, salmons were the guardians of sacred pools and wells. Salmon teaches us about determination, fluidity, and cycles. With its exhausting journey home—upstream to its spawning grounds—salmon reveals the importance of epic life-changing voyages, unstoppable progress, and the capacity to overcome great obstacles. A leap of faith can be exceedingly frightening and yet the most healing of experiences. Salmon can help us find focus for the soul, which can carry us through any turbulence. Follow salmon if you seek wisdom and inspiration, and you will be led on a journey through the depths of your soul.

Associations: Cycles, determination, healing, progress.

Sea Gull

Sea gulls seem to come in all shapes and sizes, but the quintessential is the herring gull. Stately and large, with a fifty-eight-inch wingspan, this gull is indeed a master of the wind. For centuries mariners relied on the flight line of gulls to find land—so this bird reminds us that duty and responsibility are to be gladly assumed and never shirked. Sea gull also teaches the importance of clear communication. We can gain more nuanced understanding by asking mindful questions. From sea gull we learn adaptability, helping us go with the flow when necessary, and we see how and when to clear things from our life. Through sea gull's lessons we can learn to soar to new heights, finding freedom of spirit as well as the beauty in simple things.

Associations: Communication, freedom, responsibility, simplicity.

---

9 Nathalie Ward, *Stellwagen Bank*, 108.

Seal

Stories abound concerning these playful, active creatures. The legendary selkies of Scotland were said to live most of their lives as seals, but on certain nights they came ashore, shedding their skins and turning into beautiful women. In Iceland, seals were said to come on shore on St. John's night (Midsummer, June 23) to dance on the beach.[10] Celtic people believed them to be guides for sailors and fishermen because of their link to the powers of the deep. As a guide, seal helps us center and find focus in our life. Seal's Otherworld associations aid us in maintaining the deep level of spirituality we need to keep in balance. The shy but curious nature of seal leads us to enlarge our own capacity to explore the world through our creativity.

Associations: Balance, creativity, curiosity, playfulness.

Turtle

Sea turtles spend their lives at sea, most often as solitary wanderers of the deep. Traveling hundreds of miles to lay eggs on the beach where they themselves and their ancestors before them hatched, turtles have earned the name of "ancient mariners."[11] Through this feat of navigation, turtle teaches us to pay attention and remain aware about the truly important matters in life. In Eastern mythology, turtle symbolized longevity and immortality, fertility and perseverance. Through these attributes, turtle teaches us how to awaken to opportunity—those presented to us as well as those we create for ourselves.

Associations: Fertility, immortality, longevity, opportunity, perseverance.

---

10 Bassett, *Legends and Superstitions*, 245.

11 Trish MacGregor and Millie Germondo, *Animal Totems*, 216.

Turtle

Whale

The largest creature on earth derives its name from the Norwegian word *hval,* meaning "wheel." And "wheel-like" aptly describes whale's diving motion. It also implies cycles, which are inherent in whale's migratory and musical patterns. Through these habits, whale reveals the importance of freeing our creativity and remembering to sing. Like all marine mammals, whale's rugged and adaptable ancestors left the changing environment on land about 55 million years ago for life in the sea.[12] Perhaps this fact can remind us that we can always change our lives around. Whale's sounding dive teaches us the value of exploring our inner depths. Communication and community are other areas where whale guides our focus for developing cooperation and harmony.

Associations: Communication, community, creativity, cycles, harmony.

---

12 Ward, *Stellwagen Bank,* 146, 144.

PRACTICE: THE SEA JOURNEY

The Sea Journey technique will help you find and begin working with your sea fetch. Following the narrative text given here (and ideally recorded in advance), you will enter a meditative state that lets you shift your reality away from mundane thoughts and actions and tap into the network of energy that underlies the world of our everyday consciousness. Starting on an imaginary beach, you will travel far beyond.

About the Journey Technique

Although this kind of journeying is used in spiritual practices, it is not rooted in any particular religion. It is a tool for connecting to the spirit realm. Not only does it provide access to a different reality, it also gives us a way to function there. Some may call it a trance state, expanded awareness, astral projection, ecstatic trance, or shamanic journeying. Traditional shamans have generally used these states for divination, healing, and acquiring guidance or knowledge to bring back to the conscious plane. When we balance the deep inner realm of self, we can then bring the rest of our life into balance more easily.

Our everyday awareness is a product of our physical senses. When we are journeying, subtle energy replaces those senses and we open to a new level of perception. While even daydreaming can be considered a light trance state, deeper levels can open "paranormal senses and psychic awareness." In the words of Starhawk, "Trance unlocks the tremendous potential inherent in our unused awareness. We can augment our sensitivity, growth, and creativity."[13]

Like the beach, the journeying state is an in-between place where the conscious and unconscious can touch. We open ourselves for transformation and we let submerged experiences surface. And as we noted earlier, letting go of old baggage can be liberating—but it can also be challenging. If difficulties arise, it is wise to seek professional help.

The journey technique requires no special equipment or drugs. It occurs naturally, if we let it. While it may take a little practice, it is simply

---

13 Starhawk, *The Spiral Dance*, 154, 157.

a matter of relaxing physically and then letting go of our ordinary state of consciousness—which can be aided by mesmerizing sounds such as drumming, rattling, or chanting.

Preparing for a Sea Journey

For a start, you may want to record the following Sea Journey narrative, then replay it to guide you whenever you are ready to journey.

An interlude of sound, such as drumming or rattling, can aid in your journey: consider inserting ten or fifteen minutes at the marked place in the text. Alternatively, you can use the sound recording exclusively, without recording the narrative at all. (In that case, read the narrative carefully in advance.) Recordings of drumming and rattling for meditation are widely available; each sound imparts its own quality to the journey. Which should you use? Some people find drumming more distracting than helpful in shifting levels of consciousness; they prefer the softer rattling sound. Experiment to find what suits you. I do suggest finding a recording with a "call back": a shift in rhythm that gently breaks the mesmerizing effect and helps the listener gradually return to everyday consciousness—preferable to an abrupt ending or "click."

As you read the narrative, if you find that you prefer a slightly different setting—coastal location, time of day—use that for your access point. As you repeat your journey over time, it may evolve to reflect your personal tastes and experiences. Your inner seascape comes alive as it becomes part of your world.

Your first encounter with your sea fetch may be brief, or it might last a while if your fetch chooses to relate information or show you around. Let the sea fetch set the pace. Don't try to force an agenda or demand answers to questions. Be polite and respectful, but not subservient. And don't expect great fanfare. Information is usually imparted as guidance, confirmation, or affirmation—not as true knowledge on a silver platter. Each of us must work for it, seek it, and assimilate it. If it is correct and important for you, you will know it. Over time, with familiarity, your fetch may guide you to particular sea deities or places and help you navigate personal issues.

On the practical side: take time to prepare yourself and your space, almost as if you were taking a physical journey. Give yourself plenty of time without interruption in a private, quiet place. (If you want to first create a sea circle to help build and contain the energy, do so, preparing your space as if for a sea meditation.) In daylight you may want to darken the room; at night you might light a candle or use very soft light. You can either sit in a comfortable chair or lie down. If you lie on the floor, use a pillow and a blanket or something soft underneath you; you might want to cover yourself, too. Wear comfortable, loose clothes. Think ahead to prevent any physical discomfort that might distract you. Keep your journal close by to document your journey afterward: this will also aid in the transition back to your everyday world.

Sit or lie comfortably and begin using the ocean breath to bring your focus within. When you feel sea-centered, begin the narrative.

The Sea Journey: Narrative Text

[Begin recording here.]

Listen to the gentle surf and feel yourself standing on a beach facing the water in the early morning. The light is soft, and the gentle breeze is warm. Feel your bare feet on wet sand. You hear a wave crash and the surf hiss toward the shore. Cool water washes over your feet and up to your ankles.

The water seems to pause before it reverses direction and heads out to rally the next breaker that is gathering height. You stand, listening and watching as the waves rush ashore one by one to bathe your feet. Each time a wave withdraws, you feel it take a little sand from under your feet until your toes are snuggled into the sand. Slowly draw in a deep breath of fresh air and enjoy the slight tinge of salt in your nostrils. As you listen to the sea gulls' call, you become aware of something small bumping against your ankle. Looking down, you notice a moon shell floating in the water. Bend down, retrieve it, and inspect it more closely.

A first it looks like any number of shells you've seen, but then you notice that the folds of its spiral are a deep, rich purple. As it dries in the air, the white shell turns to a sparkling pink-lavender that seems to glow in your hand. Looking up, you notice another shell several feet away. As you lengthen your gaze, you see a trail of these shells twinkling as they dry in the sand. You decide to follow them.

You walk for a few minutes, following the trail at the edge of the surf. When you glance back, you see that the shells you have passed are no longer twinkling; they simply appear ordinary. Looking forward again, the shells seem to glow in sequence, beckoning you onward. You continue to follow them over a rocky area, around several large boulders, and into an enormous sea cave. The temperature is unexpectedly warm and comfortable inside. Only part of the cave floor is covered with water, and it will be several hours before the tide begins its slow return.

Continuing, you follow the trail of shells to the back of the cave and find what appears to be a narrow doorway. Turning sideways, you fit through the passage and enter a room filled with the twinkling spiral shells. The cave walls are bathed in a soft lavender glow that draws you in. Even though you are in a strange new place, you feel at ease. A large rock next to a deep pool of water in the center of the chamber looks like an elaborately carved chair. You take a seat, close your eyes, and listen to the gentle echo of the surf outside.

As you sit there, you become aware of the presence of another being in the chamber. Allow a moment or two to feel the other's energy. Slowly open your eyes and greet the being who has come to meet you. Because sight is not our strongest sense, you may not have a clear image in front of you. Let your intuition and energy accommodate your vision.

Introduce yourself and then ask if the being is your sea fetch. If it seems appropriate, ask his or her name.

[Insert drumming or rattling audio here. Let it play for ten to fifteen minutes, then slowly lower the volume and read the remaining text.]

It is time to begin your return journey. Thank your sea fetch and offer a gift. It may be a piece of jewelry that you wear, something in your pocket, or a piece of your clothing. Give something that has value to you, and give it freely.

Now you are back in the center of the glowing chamber. The twinkling light of the moon shells begins to dim as you walk to the narrow passage. After retracing your route, pause briefly to let your eyes adjust, then step out of the sea cave onto the beach. Before rounding the bend at the large boulder, you glance back toward the cave but find that the rock face appears as a solid wall. Even so, you know that you can find the cave and your sea fetch again by following the trail of twinkling moon shells, which will always reappear when you need to find the way.

[End recording.]

After the Journey

Take your time as you cross the threshold back to your everyday world. You may feel disoriented, especially returning from your first journey. Even after later journeys, when you begin to move deeper into your inner world and spirit, you may feel slow or displaced when you come back. Journaling aids in this transition and lets you access the journey's events, sights, and conversations. Even if you do not recall it in chronological order, record as much detail as you can, either on paper or on audio, before it slips from your consciousness. During your post-journey, take time for a light snack and beverage such as herb tea.

What if nothing occurs on your first journey? That is a real possibility. If this is the case, simply accept that this may not be the time for you to meet a sea fetch. It does not mean that you never will; it is simply not the time. Don't be discouraged; try again another time.

If you have met your sea fetch, confirmation will come to you during everyday life. For example, if a dolphin has presented itself to you in the cave's pool, you will soon find dolphins in pictures, television programs, books, and elsewhere. When this happens, think: "Ah, yes, thank you for showing me," or whatever words are appropriate for you to acknowledge your fetch's signal.

———•———

Our frequency of journeying and meditating may ebb and flow like the tides, but finding our sea center will always keep us connected with source. Like a little periwinkle, we may be tossed around by life's events, but we know that something deep in our soul will guide us to where we belong. Once we enter the heart of mystery, we will never be totally lost again.

The Mythical Realm

This book would not be complete without portraying some of the myriad mythical sea creatures known to humankind. These marvelous creatures reflect the human imagination and the search to explain the unknown. Even modern marine biologists admit there is a vast, strange world in the deep ocean that is yet to be explored.

Just as people of antiquity used deities to explain the wondrous powers of the ocean, they also used sea monsters to warn of the unknown. At best, some of these sea creatures were portrayed as pranksters, but many were downright deadly—perhaps because of the unpredictable nature of the ocean and the fact that anyone caught unprepared at sea is in for trouble. Creating devilish creatures was also a way of explaining natural phenomena such as whirlpools.

Sea serpent myths can be found around the globe from Asia, India, Africa, the Mediterranean, Scandinavia, the Americas, and the northern regions of the Inuit.[14] And although not a serpent of the sea, the Loch Ness monster has given rise to a legend and a search that are very much alive. The Leviathan monster mentioned in the Bible was chaos incarnate, his massive tail roiling the seas. Indeed, the presence of a sea serpent usually caused or foretold some form of impending doom. However, this wasn't the case in China, where dragons of the various seas brought generosity and good fortune.

Indeed, not all of the mythical beings and animals of the ocean were intent on destruction. The seas were also believed to be home to a range of water sprites, fairies, and other beings. The most legendary were the mermaids. In classical myths, the quintessential beautiful mermaid often was seen seated on a rock, combing her long hair. Magic mirrors were standard features of the lore, as were their pastimes of singing and enticing

---

14 Horace Beck, *Folklore and the Sea*, 256.

sailors. The male equivalents of mermaids were also prevalent worldwide. A recorded incident with one occurred in September 1639 in Casco Bay near Portland, Maine.[15] Unlike mermaids, mermen were said to be very unattractive, with green teeth and seaweed for hair.

According to African and Caribbean legends, the mermaids called Mama Alo could transform and come ashore as cats, which is why stray cats in the West Indies were not welcome guests.[16] Despite many stories portraying mer-people as dangerous, they often proved helpful, guiding ships out of precarious situations. In general, mer-people epitomized the mystery of the ocean realm and the human search for something beyond the visible world.

Sea deities and beings were adept shape-shifters and frequently took the guise of seals. The roanes of Ireland and Scotland and the selkies of the Orkney Islands could shed their seal skins to go ashore in human form. Stealing their seal garb gave a person power over them because returning to the sea was impossible without it. But however long this being stayed ashore—perhaps even marrying a human and having children— the pull of the sea was so great that the quest to return was never forgotten. In almost all of the legends that goal was achieved.

In Homer's *Odyssey*, the ancient Greek hero encountered a different form of dangerous sea monster: the whirlpool. Like other whirlpools, this one (known as Charybdis) had a partner in crime in the form of dangerous shoals (called Scylla). By naming them, the Greeks had also endowed them with human characteristics such as anger and evil intent. In contrast, Norse mythology referred to whirlpools as "the boiling kettle of [the sea god] Hymer."[17]

---

15 William Willis, *The History of Portland*, 60–61.

16 Beck, *Folklore and the Sea*, 250–251.

17 Bassett, *Legends and Superstitions*, 20.

Mythical Sea Creatures and Beings

Adaro—Solomon Islands. A warlike type of merman with gills and webbed feet.

Aegeon—Greece. A monster with fifty heads and a hundred arms, personifying hurricanes and violent seas. He was also known as Briareus and could have been an aspect of Poseidon.

Ahi Budhnya—India (Hindu). A serpent of the deep primeval waters.

Alcina / Fata Alcina—Italy. A monster who lived in the Straits of Messina. Sailors who saw her drowned.

Ao-Jun—China. A dragon of the western sea that brought good fortune.

Ao-K'in—China. A dragon of the southern sea that brought goodness.

Ao-Kuang—China. A dragon of the eastern sea that brought virtue.

Ao-Shun—China. A dragon of the northern sea that brought generosity.

Aonbarr—Isle of Man. The magical horse of sea god Manannan that could travel through the ocean or over land.

Ao-Jun

Ben Varrey—Isle of Man. A mermaid who, depending on her mood, lured sailors to their death or warned them of approaching bad weather.

Blue Men of the Minch—Scotland. Water fairies who roiled the waters of the Minch Channel near the Outer Hebrides. Their leader was called Shony. The Blue Men were described as having wings and a fondness for singing. They were said to board ships and demand tribute. If they were not appeased, they would cause storms. On the Isle of Skye, the Blue Men were believed to be remnants of the Picts, who painted their bodies with blue woad.[18]

Bonito Maidens—Solomon Islands. Mermaids.

Brounger—Scotland. A type of water fairy who inhabited the sea along the east coast of Scotland and warned of approaching storms.

Bucca Gwidden—Cornwall, England. Offerings of food and drink were made to this water fairy to bring good luck. Originally a sea god, his name means "white spirit."[19]

Cabbyl Ushty—Isle of Man. A type of fairy horse of the sea, distinguishable by its backward hooves. Humans who tried to ride these creatures were usually drowned.

Ceasg—Scotland. A mermaid that would lure sailors to their deaths but who, if caught, was bound to deliver three wishes. She was also known as the Maiden of the Wave.[20]

Charybdis—Greece. A whirlpool in the Straits of Messina that could consume entire ships. Along with her companion Scylla, Charybdis attacked Odysseus and his crew on their legendary voyage. She was also known as the Witch of the Shoals.[21]

---

18 Beck, *Folklore and the Sea*, 242.

19 Franklin, *Illustrated Encyclopedia of Fairies*, 38–39.

20 Ibid., 46.

21 Jobes, *Dictionary of Mythology*, 316.

Coirebhreacain—Scotland. Also known as Cailleach the Hag. Located between Jura and Scarba, the Cailleach made it a gamble to use the shortcut through the Crinan Canal (an alternative to passing around the Mùll of Kintyre). It has been said that "the roar of the whirlpool can be heard a distance of twenty miles and the confused seas attain a height of twenty feet."[22]

Daoine Mara—Scotland. The Gaelic name for a type of mer-people, which literally translates as "sea people." In oral tradition, some Scottish clans were known as the People of the Sea.[23]

Davy Jones—England. An ocean spirit or ghost. Sailors lost at sea were said to have gone to Davy Jones' Locker at the bottom of the deep.

Dopkalfar—Norway. Dark elves that lived in either the woods or the sea.

Each-Uisge—Scotland. A fairy water horse that lived in the sea as well as the lochs.

Fée des Houles—Brittany, France. Sea fairies that made their homes in caves.

Fiachra—Ireland. The king of the western sea fairies.

Fin-Folk—Scotland. There are extensive legends about the Fin-Folk who were variously known as Finn-Men, Muckle Men, Fion, and Fin Finn, which meant small.[24] As little boat people they were later associated with Finland. Through the name Fion, they were linked with Ireland's legendary hero Fion the Fair and associated with the Otherworld. In some areas of Scotland they were believed to be sea fairies with beautiful gardens around their underwater homes. (In Cornwall and Wales, too, they were called sea gardeners.) Elsewhere in Scotland they were seen as the remnants of the ancient Pict people. Sightings were recorded from 1682 to 1864. They were also called Finn Wizards in Shetland, where they were

22 Beck, *Folklore and the Sea*, 46.
23 MacEowen, *The Mist-Filled Path*, 37.
24 Beck, *Folklore and the Sea*, 222.

believed to don seal skins and masquerade as seals.[25] They had power over the winds through magic worked with leather bags and black strings. By unknotting the strings or unstopping the bags, they could bring up a wind and cause a storm. Belief in the Fin-Folk also stretched to Norway, where they were said to keep crows as familiars who would let them know what was going on in the world.[26] Only the Fin-Folk could ride a water horse.

Gioga—Scotland. The queen of the sea trows (trolls) who were mainly found around the islands.

Grendel—Norway. A giant monster that frequently devastated the North Sea coast. He personified the powers of the deep sea and storm floods. Grendel was killed by Beowulf.

Groach Vor—Brittany, France and Cornwall, England. A type of mermaid.

Gwenhidwy—Wales. A shepherdess mermaid. The foamy waves were called her sheep and the ninth wave her ram. The Welsh believed that one should take shelter when her flocks were being driven to shore.

Haaf-fish—Orkney Islands, Scotland. A type of selkie.

Hakenmann—Germany. A monster of coastal North Germany that had the head of a man and body of a fish.

Halfway People—Canada. The Micmac name for mer-people. In their legends, the mermaids sang to warn fishermen of storms.

Havfine—Norway. Mermaids that were bad omens.

Havfrue—Denmark. A mermaid who could be a friend or a foe to fishermen, as her presence foretold of coming storms. She gathered the bones of those who drowned.

Havmand—Denmark. A handsome type of merman who was friendly to humans.

---

25 Bassett, *Legends and Superstitions*, 106.

26 Beck, *Folklore and the Sea*, 224.

Kelpie

Jormungandr—Norway. A great serpent that circled the human world with his tail in his mouth. He personified the ocean that was believed to circle Middle Earth. It was also known as the Midgard serpent.

Juruta / Jurute—Lithuania. A mermaid or sea fairy that originated as a sea goddess and consort of Perun, the god of thunder. She is associated with the gemstone amber.

Kakamora—Solomon Islands. Cave-dwelling ocean fairies known for their long, sharp fingernails. They were said to have an aversion to the color white.

Kami—Japan (Shinto). Elementals living under the ocean.

Karawatoniga—Malaysia. Seashore fairies known for their beautiful hair.

Kelpie—Scotland. Also known as Nix, Nuggle, water horse, water bull, and *Each Uisage* (Gaelic), this creature was considered the "most ancient and primitive type of the mermaid's northern ancestors."[27] The most common form of the Kelpie was a gray water horse that offered rides and then

---

27 Ibid., 236.

threw its passenger into the water, sometimes to drown. Kelpies could appear as human men, but had hair of seaweed. When not throwing riders, they liked to stand atop water wheels, bringing them to a halt.

Kraken—Scandinavia. A round, flat sea creature that created whirlpools to ensnare passing ships. In other legends it was variously portrayed as a giant fish, whale, or squid.

Lakhmu—Babylon. A sea monster called up by Tiamat to fight against the god Marduk.

Lamia—Greece. Sea fairies whose dancing could create waterspouts.

Leviathan—Phoenicia. A sea serpent/dragon that came into being on the fifth day of creation. As chaos incarnate, his great tail made the seas roil. His name means "coiled."[28]

Luchorpáin—Ireland. A type of leprechaun that could live beneath the sea. They allowed humans to safely journey to their realm by use of a magic cloak over their heads or special herbs placed in their ears.

Maighdean Mara—Scotland. A mermaid whose name means "sea maiden."[29]

Maighdean na Tuinne—Scotland. A mermaid whose name means "maiden beneath the waves."[30]

Mal-de-mer—Cornwall, England and Brittany, France. Sea fairies that caused shipwrecks, then took possession of the drowned souls. Their name means "evil of the sea."[31]

Mama Alo—African and Caribbean. Also called Mama Jo, these mermaids liked to capture a person's shadow—metaphor for soul. They could transform and come ashore as cats, which is why stray cats in the West Indies were not welcome guests.[32]

---

28 Cotterell and Storm, *Ultimate Encyclopedia of Mythology*, 293.

29 Franklin, *Illustrated Encyclopedia of Fairies*, 168.

30 Ibid.

31 Ibid.

32 Beck, *Folklore and the Sea*, 250–251.

Mära-Halddo—Lapland. A type of sea fairy.

Mara-Warra—Ireland. Mermaids with rich undersea dwellings.

Margygr—Greenland. Mer-folk.

Marie Morgane—British Isles. Mermaids related to Celtic fairies.

Mari-morgan—Brittany, France. Sea fairies usually described as sitting on rocks and combing their luxuriant hair with golden combs.

Marmaeler—Scandinavia. Children of the Meerweiber.

Mary Player—England. A mermaid who could cause a ship to sink by swimming three circles around it.

Meerfrauen / Meerjungfern—Germany. Mermaids.

Meermann—Germany. Merman.

Meerminnen—Netherlands. Mermaid.

Meerweiber—Scandinavia. Mermaids or sea women.

Mer-Folk—Legends abound worldwide about these near-mortal beings who lived mainly under water in a fairylike paradise. They occasionally came ashore disguised as humans through the use of a magical garment such as a veil, cap, scarf, or sometimes a seal skin (such as in the legends of selkies).[33] Capturing such a garment gave control over a mer-person.

Mermaids—Classical mythology often depicted mermaids seated on rocks combing their long hair. They were voluptuously human above the waist with the lower body of a fish. In worldwide legends their personalities vary from helpful to malevolent.

Mermen—The male equivalent of mermaids, also called Tritons. Unlike mermaids, mermen were said to be very unattractive.

Merrow / Morvadh / Murrughach—Gaelic names for the mer-folk. They were portrayed as peaceful and sometimes intermarried with humans. The offspring of such a union had webbed toes and fingers.

---

33 Ibid., 230–231.

Merrymaids—Cornwall, England. Mermaids.

Mer-woman / Mer-wife—England. Mermaids.

Muireartach / Muilearteach—Scotland. A type of sea fairy that appeared as an old woman with blue-gray skin and one eye. She could also appear as a sea serpent and cause storms.

Murdhuachas—Ireland. Sea fairies with the head of a seal or walrus. Sometimes they helped sailors; at other times they hindered them.

Mweedn—Wales. A child of the sea.

Naga Padoha—Southeast Asia. A sea serpent that tried to destroy the first lands created by the god Batara Guru.

Neagle / Nuggle / Nyaggle—Shetland Islands, Scotland. Alternate names for a water horse.

Nickur / Nykur / Ninnir—Iceland. A gray or black water horse also found in rivers and lakes.

Ningyo—Japan. A mermaid.

Nuckelavee—Scotland. A sea fairy that usually appeared as a grotesque water horse. While it could go ashore, it had an aversion to fresh water and rain.

Orc—Italy (Roman). A sea monster.

Polong—New Zealand. Sea fairies that fought with the Maori people.

Roane—Ireland and Scotland. Sea fairies that took the form of seals. Onshore they could remove the seal skin, but anyone who took possession of it had power over the roane.

Ryu-wo—Japan. A sea dragon that was also king of rain and storms.

Scylla—Greece. The six-headed rock monster of the Straits of Messina. According to legends she was a sea nymph who Circe turned into a monster, jealous of her trysts with Zeus and Poseidon. Along with her companion, Charybdis the whirlpool, Scylla attacked Odysseus and his crew on their legendary voyage.

Ningyo

Sea serpents—Legends of great unknown creatures have been reported worldwide through the ages. One recorded incident in New England occurred off Cape Ann, Massachusetts, in June 1639.[34]

Sea sprites—Isle of Man. Sea fairies who used discarded seashells for boats. They usually aided people in need.

Sea trows—Northern Europe, Scandinavia, British Isles. A type of troll living at the bottom of the ocean. While they tended to play tricks on people, they were not malevolent.

Selkie—Orkney Islands, Scotland. Sea fairies that appeared as seals, but shed the disguise on land. They came ashore to dance for special occasions. As with roanes, stealing a selkie's seal skin gave a person power over it. Various legends portrayed selkies as fallen angels or humans who were guilty of major transgressions. Male selkies were said to take human lovers.

Shoopiltees—Orkney and Shetland Islands, Scotland. Water ponies.

---

34 Ibid.

Usumgal

Sirena—Guam. A mermaid who could only be caught with a net of human hair.

Tangie—Shetland Islands, Scotland. A mischievous type of water horse.

Tarroo-Ushtey—Isle of Man. A dangerous water bull that was capable of going ashore.

Uilebheist—Orkney and Shetland Islands, Scotland. A sea monster/dragon with multiple heads.

Undines—Greece. Sea fairies whose name means "wave."[35] They could appear as human or sea horse. Elementals of any type of water came to be called undines.

Usumgal—Sumer. A sea serpent.

Vatea—Polynesia. A mermaid that was half porpoise.

Water bull—Scotland. Similar to a water horse; however, it protected people from harm rather than playing tricks on them.

---

35 Franklin, *Illustrated Encyclopedia of Fairies*, 259.

Water horse—Scotland. Also called a kelpie. A horse with a wheel for a tail, linking it to symbols for both the sun and "the edge of night."[36] Before it disappeared below the sea, a tiny blue flame could be seen. On the east coast of the Shetland Islands the water horse was a light color, and on the west coast it was dark with sand in its mane. In contrast to the kelpie legends, the Shetland water horse could take riders to a beautiful realm under the sea. The journey was pleasant but the rider could not return to the world of humans.

Waternöme—Germany. Mermaid or sea-woman.

Wihwin—Central America. A water horse that spent its summers in the forested mountains.

Zabel—Phoenicia. A creature known as a lord of the sea, he was summoned to fight against Baal.

JOURNAL QUESTIONS

1. Describe the sensations you experienced with the sea journey.

2. Has a sea fetch made itself known to you? If so, how?

3. What do you believe its significance is for you?

4. Has working with a fetch, along with your other Sea Magic work, aided you in finding or furthering your inner path?

---

36 Beck, *Folklore and the Sea*, 236.

VI

THE MOON, MEDITATIONS, AND EVERYDAY LIFE

You must not only become receptive to
having guidance available to you to
manifest your human intentions, but
you must be receptive to giving this
energy back to the world.

WAYNE DYER
The Power of Intention

TODAY, AS IN THE PAST, the moon and the sea are sources of mystery and fascination. The moon is a glowing circle in the sky and the ocean a blue circle around the earth. The circular tides of energy move continually through the heavens, the sea, and our body, connecting us with the universe and making us children of the cosmos and of the cosmic sea. With the sea centering practice that we learned at the beginning of this book, we can move a circle of energy through us and around us. From the heart center we connect with all that is.

THE MOON-SEA CONNECTION

Astrology began with the observation that "the moon was directly responsible for the ebb and flow of the tides," according to Thomas Dietrich.[1] Aristotle believed that "the mysterious pulsations of the ocean" were caused by the sun moving the winds of the earth, while Pytheas attributed the tides to the moon.[2] The Greeks were not the only people who saw a connection between the moon and the tides. The Celts, the Inuit, and the peoples of India, China, Japan, and New Zealand all observed the cyclical rhythms. In the South Pacific, the Polynesians linked their moon goddess Hina with the sea by calling her Lady of the Ocean Waves.[3]

---

1 Thomas Deitrich, *The Origin of Culture and Civilization*, 187.
2 Bassett, *Legends and Superstitions*, 27.
3 Cashford, *Moon*, 79.

Shakespeare's Hamlet spoke of the moon as "the moist star upon whose influence Neptune's empire stands"(Act 1, Scene 1). In thirteenth-century Italy, the Florentine philosopher Brunetto Latini put forth the notion that waves were caused "by the efforts of the earth to breathe." The Shetland Islanders north of Scotland believed that the waves were created by monsters, while in Indonesia people imagined that a giant crab's movements pushed the waters ashore.[4]

After Isaac Newton sorted out the issue of gravity, the movement of the tides was finally understood. It could be explained through the combined effects of the gravitational pull of the sun and the moon. The tides have two daily highs and two daily lows: the tide is "in" twice and "out" twice. Each tide takes just over six hours to complete—a cycle of two high and low tides takes about twenty-four hours and fifty minutes. That fifty-minute lag is the moon's influence. If the sun's gravitational pull were the only factor, the tides would follow a twenty-four-hour solar day, with high and low tides occurring at the same time every day. But the moon's pull means the tides occur at different times each day, progressing gradually around the clock.

The tides also follow a longer cycle, with extra-high and extra-low points, depending on the phase of the moon. A spring tide occurs during the full and new moons—that is, about every two weeks—when the sun, earth, and moon are more or less in a straight line.[5] It is also known as a moon tide.[6] At this time the difference between high and low tides is greater than at other times; the "tidal range" is wider. The high tides are higher and the low tides are lower. (In this case the word *spring*, rather than referring to a season, harkens back to its Old English meaning, "to grow or swell."[7])

Neap tides occur during the first and third quarters of the moon, when the sun, earth, and moon form a right-angled triangle. During these times

---

4 Bassett, *Legends and Superstitions*, 28.

5 Sam Hinton, *Seashore Life of Southern California*, 18.

6 David Ross, *The Fisherman's Ocean*, 35.

7 Hinton, *Seashore Life of Southern California*, 19.

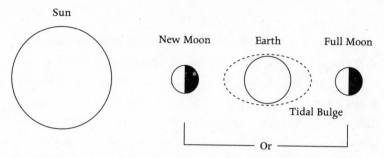

Spring tide celestial alignment

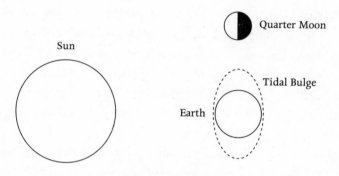

Neap tide celestial alignment

the tidal range is narrower. The name for this tide also comes from the Old English, meaning "scarce."[8]

Another connection between the moon and the sea is the widely accepted theory that the moon was once part of the earth: as the earth was being formed, it was hit by a roving planetoid that dislodged a huge amount of material which, as it orbited the earth, eventually formed the moon.[9] As Rachel Carson noted, "The next time you stand on a beach at night, watching the moon's bright path across the water, and conscious of the moon-drawn tides, remember that the moon itself may have been born of a great tidal wave of earthly substance, torn off into space."[10]

8 Ibid.

9 William Hartman, *Moon Origin*, 579.

10 Carson, *Sea Around Us*, 10.

THE RHYTHM OF LIFE

The rhythm and pull of the tides are so strong that some marine animals, after being removed from the sea, maintain their tide-coincident daily behavior patterns as though they were still exposed to the ocean.[11] Just as the tides and moon wax and wane, so too does our energy ebb and flow. Although women are most obviously in tune with monthly cycles, post-menopausal women as well as men experience monthly rhythms. By tuning into these patterns, we can bring new awareness and insight into our lives. Instead of working against our natural rhythms we can relax into them and enjoy who we are.

By expanding our awareness of the natural world, we can coordinate our meditation or prayers with the greater flow of tidal and lunar energy, which can enhance and amplify our intentions. Dr. Wayne Dyer noted that "meditation allows you to make conscious contact with your Source and regain the power of intention."[12]

The rising tide and waxing moon are times of sending forth, of gaining energy and growth. Meditating on achieving your goals during these times can strengthen your intent and the probability that they will manifest. For this purpose, create a symbol to focus on by placing a representative object on your altar. For example, if your goal is to further your education or study for an exam, place a pearl (pearls of wisdom) on your altar. If your intent is to draw prosperity to you, a pearl or cowry shell (once used as currency) can act as a symbol. Use any type of seashell with associations that correspond to your intention.

The ebbing tide and waning moon are periods of decrease and removal. There are times when we want or need to release things from our lives, and this is a good opportunity to express that intent. For example, if a relationship is ending or you are working to resolve a problem, dissolve some sea salt in water to represent a decrease or lessening. If you are near the shore, go to the water's edge, taking along a shell that represents the issue. Hold it in your hands as you visualize the problem or person, then

---

11 Carson, *Edge of the Sea*, 51.

12 Dyer, *Power of Intention*, 64.

toss the shell into the ocean. Feel the burden lifted and know that Mother Ocean aids you with healing energy. If you are disposing of bad habits or anything negative, the sea will neutralize and cleanse the energy.

PRACTICE: COSMIC SEA CENTERING

Try this sea centering exercise in the light of the moon, expanding your awareness to the cosmic powers of the moon and tides.

The moon and the sea provide solace and serenity for the soul. Moonlight parts the darkness just enough for the eyes to reassure the mind of our physical location. The moon casts a magical sheen across our world, letting us see things differently—perhaps only what is necessary to see. Without the sun's glare it is easier to journey into the stillness of the soul. The ocean also aids in this journey, her rhythm bringing us to an active stillness. In any sea centering exercise, outwardly we are not moving, but on the inside an entire ocean—our personal ocean—is flowing. When we can focus solely on this energy even for a moment, we glimpse our true essence. As we practice this active stillness—our sea stillness— we come to know who we are. Stripped bare of all the judgments placed on us by others and ourselves, we can reach the core of simply being. And there we discover joy. It may seem strange at first, because we grow up learning that happiness is found only through things or other people. But underneath all the stories we've been told, underneath all our experience, joy is right here inside us. It is easy to miss if we live haphazardly, letting too many unimportant things crowd our days.

You don't have to be outdoors to do a cosmic sea centering; a chair by a window that receives moonlight will do nicely. Or open the curtains and blinds and allow only moonlight to brighten the room you are in—no candles or electric light. Let just the silvery glow illuminate your world. Needless to say, sitting on a beach in the moonlight would be ideal, but it's not necessary, because you have been cultivating your connection with Mother Ocean. No matter how far from her you may be, you can connect with her energy.

Prepare your space and yourself as usual. In a cosmic sea centering you are establishing a circle of energy: you, the ocean, and the moon.

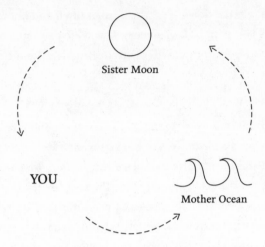

The energy flow of a cosmic sea centering is circular.

Begin centering as you usually do, connecting with your internal ocean. Then continue to think of your energy expanding and linking with the rhythm of the waves. As the tide washes the shore, so too does the universal energy ebb and flow through your body. Listen for the sounds of the ocean; they will echo in your mind.

Expand your awareness to the energy pouring down from the heavens. Imagine the moonlight moving to the same ebb and flow that you feel within. When you have reached that point, further expand your senses to encompass an energetic circle: the moon pulls on the energy of the ocean, which pulls your energy. You, in turn, pull the energy of the moon. Your sea centering energy grows exponentially as it moves through you, the sea, and the moon.

You may have the sensation of dissolving boundaries, as though your body has no beginning or end. This feeling may seem precarious at first, but trust in yourself. Surrender to the sensation of being at one with the universe. The experience may be brief—a mere flicker—but your mind and body will remember it.

Slowly bring your awareness back into the room (or beach) where you are sitting. Bring your awareness back into your body as you return to a sea centering flow of your own energy. After one circuit, sit in stillness and silence. You may find that you are smiling.

PRACTICE: FIND BALANCE WITH THE EQUINOX TIDES

Every year, two extra-high tides occur: one at the full moon near the spring equinox (around March 21) and one at the new moon near the autumn equinox (around September 23). The equinox is a time of balance when day and night, light and dark are equal. As a result, these are powerful times for finding personal balance.

Prepare for meditation with whatever altar setup works best for you. Include two seashells that can hold water. Place a little seawater in one and leave the other empty. Gather enough other shells of any type; you will use these to create a circle on the floor around your altar. When you are ready, start with the Equinox Tide Call and then begin making the circle of shells. When it's finished, take a seat in front of your altar within the circle.

Do your sea centering, then take a few minutes to feel its effects. Begin to visualize the global ocean coming into balance with the energy of the equinox. Take the water-filled shell and pour half the water into the other shell to create a symbol of balance. Feel your energy coming into alignment and balance with the earth and sea. Stay with your sensations for as long as they feel flowing and natural, then end the meditation.

The Equinox Tide Call

Equal are the light and dark,
With these shells, a circle I mark.
Moon above, raise the sea,
Shine and flow, bring balance to me.

In acknowledging the equinoxes this way, you are expanding your Sea Magic from an inner-ocean circle to a cosmic sea that also forms a sacred circle through the wheel of the year. As we come into balance at the equinoxes, we create a deep and lasting connection with the sacred world.

PRACTICE: SEASHELL MEDITATION

Although considered by some to be a Buddhist practice, meditation is a tool used in many spiritual traditions. These practices have been increasing in popularity in recent years. Texts found in 1945 at Nag Hammadi in Upper Egypt describe techniques of spiritual discipline that are not unlike Buddhist or Hindu practices designed to achieve enlightenment.[13] Like the *Yoga Sutras* of Patanjali, the text called *Zostrianos* emphasized removing physical desires, reducing the chaos of the mind, and stilling it with meditation. Likewise, Yogananda called meditation "the science of being actively calm."[14] He considered daydreaming and sleeping to be forms of passive calmness.

Meditation techniques encompass a wide variety of spiritual orientations. They include koan meditation, yoga, tai chi, ecstatic prayer, Hindu and Christian mysticism, the Western mystery schools, and the Kabbalah. In general terms, meditation has two intertwining strands: the search for the divine and the search for true inner self. Whatever its form or details, meditation involves spiritual and personal transformation.

Finding what works best for you can be an interesting and rewarding journey. As we learn to focus the mind, over time it becomes like a Möbius strip—a circle created by a strip of paper or metal that has been twisted once before the ends are joined, so that the inner surface flows onto the outer surface and vice versa. In meditation we move inward but eventually connect to the world outside. The sacredness of nature can also be found within us. We just need to take the time for stillness.

This inward and outward flow occurs as we cultivate focus and mindfulness. Malcolm Eckel suggests the "deliberate cultivation of mental image."[15] In a commentary on Yoga Sutra 1:39, Pandit Rajmani Tigunait suggests that by meditating on an object of choice one can attain "steadiness of mind." He also recommends that one use "wise selection" in the choice

---

13 Pagels, *Gnostic Gospels*, 135.

14 Paramahansa Yogananda, *Inner Peace*, 19.

15 Malcolm David Eckel, *Buddhism*, 60.

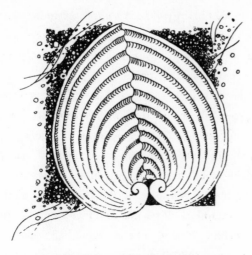

A cockle shell resembles hands at prayer.

of objects to focus on.[16] When we use seashells for focus we physically connect with an object that has been cleansed by the ocean and touched by the salt of wisdom. Energetically, we link with the shell's own properties as well as the vastness of the sea. By carefully selecting a shell, we can direct our energy and intention to where it is needed or where we want it to go.

Begin seashell meditation by preparing your altar. Clear everything from it except for a few items such as shell of seawater, a candle, and the shell that will serve as your focus. These are your starting point. Since each person's (and seashell's) energy is unique, your experience will change over time as you work with shells.

For this meditation, choose a shell for its calming and centering properties. In the example we'll use a cockle shell. The cockle appears heart-shaped when viewed from the side with its hinge joint pointing up. Turn it upside down and it resembles a pair of praying hands. For this meditation, one or both halves of the shell work equally well.

16 Pandit Rajmani Tigunait, *The Yoga Sutras*, Yoga International, 52–53.

Create a sea circle of energy, if that is appropriate for you, then spend a few minutes on a sea centering to bring your energy into line for the purpose of meditation. Hold the seashell between your palms in whichever direction is comfortable for you.

The cockle's energy brings balance and love. Focus your mind on these properties. Your eyes can be closed or focused in a soft gaze on a candle. Breathe deeply and slowly. You may be aware of energy between your hands; you may feel that the shell is no longer there. If you enjoy the tactile sensation of the shell, your energetic connection with it may begin to pulse. Whatever physical sensations occur, keep your mind focused on thoughts of balance and love. If balance and love are things that you want to increase in your life, visualize them as white light emanating from the cockle. Imagine this soft light flowing into your hands and up your arms, then surrounding your entire body.

Hold the image of this light in your mind's eye until it begins to fade. When it does, let it dissolve; don't try to force it to remain. Sit for a few moments in the experience, then release it. If you keep a journal, this is a good time to write your entry before all sensations fade from memory. End your meditation session in your usual way.

PRACTICE: HEART CHAKRA MEDITATION

Accessing the chakras, the body's seven energy centers, is a powerful way to focus our energy and come into balance with the natural world. The body's lower three chakras are self-oriented, engaging our instincts about survival, sex, and courage. When we add the fourth chakra, the heart, our energy begins to move out of these basic needs into the world. It is the fulcrum that balances the three lower chakras, our foundation, with the three higher ones, which are associated with expression, intuition, and spirituality.

The heart chakra is our place of love and compassion. The experience it brings is acceptance of all life as well as trust. From it we can be free from expectations and judgment. Its message is "I love." By activating and moving this energy we share our love and compassion with others and, on a larger scale, the entire planet.

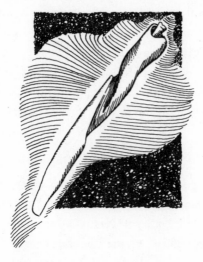

The columella is the heart of a shell.

The cockle shell works well for this meditation, too. Another option is the heart of a whelk or conch—the central column or columella. Sometimes these shells get so battered that only the heart is left, the axial pillar around which the shell's whorls formed. I have one columella that has been worn smooth. The section that was near the shell's aperture has a beautiful pattern of colors that fade to white. A columella often fits comfortably into the hand. And as we have noted, broken shells have a special power of their own.

For a heart meditation, choose your shell, then prepare yourself and your altar and space as described in the seashell meditation. When you begin to visualize light emanating from the shell, imagine it as soft pink light. Quietly chant the seed sound of the heart chakra: *Yum—Yum—Yum.* (Although this syllable is often spelled *Yam,* it is pronounced *Yum.*) A seed sound gets the energy of the chakra moving.

Continue chanting as you visualize the pink light moving up your arms to your heart. Feel the energy build as the light expands and brightens around your heart. When you feel that it has reached its peak, shift your chant to the chakra vowel sound of *Ay* (it rhymes with *bay*) to send your love and compassion out to the world. Even though you are sending energy out, you will not be depleted because by drawing energy from the shell—ultimately from the sea and the universe—you are tapping into an infinite source. You may also want to direct your energy to Mother Ocean, sending her your love and gratitude for the gifts she provides.

When it feels appropriate, bring your chanting to an end and slowly close your meditation session in your usual manner.

PRACTICE: SEASHELL MUDRA MEDITATION

Mudras are hand positions used in yoga and other meditative practices. In the most familiar mudra, the hands rest on the lap, thumb and index finger forming a circle, other fingers pointing upward. It's called *Jhana*. The thumb represents the divine, the index finger is our human consciousness, and the upward fingers show openness to receive. The hands embody the state of consciousness that we seek. Many practitioners believe that the hands are a mirror for the body and mind. Thus, mudras affect us on the physical, mental, emotional, and spiritual levels.[17]

Such gestures are not always called mudras, and they are not unique to Indian and Asian cultures. Watch a Christian priest saying Mass or a Pagan leading a ritual, and you will see formalized hand positions and gestures that symbolically project intention. On a mundane level, crossing our fingers to make a wish is another form of using our hands to send out our intentions.

In Sea Magic we use what is called *Shankh*, the shell mudra. It is commonly used in Hindu temples where the blowing of a conch shell heralds morning worship.[18] With this mudra we create the symbol of a conch shell with our hands.

Once you have prepared your space and altar and you are comfortably seated, begin by wrapping the fingers of your right hand around your left thumb. Bring your right thumb and left-hand fingers together into a peak. Don't squeeze or hold your hands rigid. Keeping them relaxed will

---

17 Gertrud Hirschi, *Mudras: Yoga in Your Hands*, 2.

18 Ibid., 76.

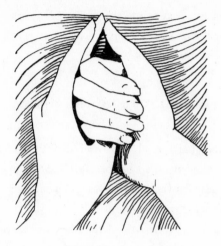

The shell, or conch, mudra

let you comfortably hold the mudra while you meditate. Position your hands in front of your heart or slightly lower.

You can keep a soft gaze on your hands or close your eyes. Chant the sound of *Om* three times, then begin using the ocean breath. Relax into the sound. If you want, visualize ocean waves. Let the meditation flow. If other thoughts intrude, bring your attention back to the sea. When it feels appropriate, bring the meditation to an end by chanting *Om* once and then remain in silence until you are ready to make the transition back to everyday awareness.

If you find that your hands get tired while holding the mudra, switch them to the prayer position—palms together, fingertips pointing up. You can keep them there, or return to the mudra when you are ready, or simply rest your hands palms upward in your lap. In any case, return to the mudra briefly at the end to chant *Om*. Using mudras will become easier over time, and you will find your hands responding to the energy. By using the shell mudra along with the ocean breath, you are evolving gently away from the sensory objects you used while learning sea centering.

For a change of pace, instead of meditating at your altar, make a circle with seashells on the floor and sit in the middle. This is also wonderful to do at the beach. Face the ocean and make the shell mudra. Simply breathe

and watch the waves. I have found that when I'm stressed, using this mudra and connecting with ocean energy is a great way to break the cycle
rather than letting it spiral out of control.

In and Around the House

Oceanariums

This is hardly an original idea, but it's one I like to use for special groups
of shells. Oceanariums are displays of sand and shells that can include
marine life such as starfish and sea horses. They can be assembled in various ways and for various purposes.

One approach is to place several shells together that are interesting as
a group—perhaps several of a particular type you are fond of. You might
use a glass jar or bowl or simply place them on a bed of sand. If you are
using a wide bowl, you can create a still life or beach vignette. With a tall,
narrow glass container, you can partially fill it with sand and then push a
few shells into it along the sides so they are visible even though covered
over with sand.

Another approach is to gather items from one place. I know a couple
who liked to spend their vacations at tropical beach resorts. In addition
to photos, they always brought home a handful of sand and shells, which
they arranged in attractive glass jars, each labeled with its location. Over
the years they amassed a collection that was fascinating to browse. Of
course, your sources need not be exotic. Any items gathered on an enjoy-
able beach outing will carry good memories and energy.

A third type of oceanarium holds shells with personal symbolic value.
The two sand dollars I found years apart, for example—I felt the need to
put them together with other shells that symbolized my healing journey.
These included a shell from Ireland (a catalyst), a couple of small cowries
(representing the oracle and birthing into my new life), and a few others
I was led to include but whose significance I have yet to figure out. Shells
that come to you with a message can make a meaningful oceanarium that
will serve as a reminder whenever you see it.

A Sea Garden

If you already have a garden, you may want to create a quiet place there to sit for meditation. An outdoor altar with shells can be a fabulous place for sea centerings, especially in the light of a full moon. If you don't have the privacy, or you need to be low-key in front of neighbors, a small bench ringed by seashells can seem unremarkable and yet be energetically powerful.

If space and privacy permit, consider laying a five- or six-foot-wide spiral of shells—a labyrinth for walking meditations. Lay the shells in a narrow spiraling path (moon snail shells are especially potent used this way). When using the spiral, walk slowly and meditatively into the center, then take time to sit or stand in stillness. Using the shell mudra and ocean breath can deepen the experience. When your meditation feels complete, turn around and slowly follow the path back out of the spiral.

An outdoor sacred space is a treasure whether it's a small place to sit, a shell circle, or a larger spiral. If you live in a coastal area, you might be able to plant your garden with dune grasses or beach heather. Otherwise, think in terms of ocean colors for leaves, grasses, and flowers. Several shades of greens and blue flowers crested by a band or two of white flowers can evoke breaking waves.

A shell circle can represent the full moon if you surround it with plants that have silvery or pale green leaves such as lamb's ear (*Stachys lanata*), "dusty miller" (*Senecio cinerama*), or chamomile (*Anthemis nobilis* or *Matricaria chamomilla*). Chamomile has light green leaves and small white daisylike flowers throughout the summer and into the autumn. In addition to its visual beauty and lovely scent, as a medicinal herb it lends a healing aspect to your circle. A simple ring of white flowers works well, too. With a little research it is easy to determine which plants will work best in your area.

Urban gardeners can place a few seashells around the base of potted house plants. And a plant stand with several tiered shelves can provide ample space for a wave-like array of small plants. An expanding seashell collection can share space with the flowerpots. Use your imagination and experiment with indoor and outdoor areas.

COLLECTING SEASHELLS

A seashell collection is easy to start, and it doesn't have to be large or exotic. As we have noted, an "ordinary" shell carries as much power as any other. Shells don't have to be perfect or whole, either. Beauty is in the eye (and energy) of the beholder. If a shell or a fragment is lovely to you, that's all that matters. A bowl of fragments is also beautiful and energetically powerful. As we have seen, the columella or central pillar of a gastropod can be exquisite. To me, the columella is the shell's heart, and its energy is strong. It symbolizes an inward journey to source, where what remains is pure soul.

Whatever types of shells you are interested in collecting, consider the three ways to obtain them: gather them yourself, trade with other people, or buy them.

Gathering shells can be a solitary meditative experience or simple fun shared with family and friends. Listening to the ocean and inhaling sea air make it a healthy endeavor as well. Picking up shells along a beach is a relaxing pastime that easily brings us into the present moment. Our attention becomes so focused that time seems nonexistent; or at least time doesn't matter. (Because of this, it's important to know the time of the tides. In some places the difference between high and low tide can be significant, and the incoming tidal flow can be very fast.)

Seashells can be found worldwide in most types of environments, and in three distinct habitat ranges. The intertidal range is the band between the high- and low-tide lines. These are the shells that wash up onto the beach or tidal pools. The subtidal range runs from the low-tide line down to the continental slope. These shells we can collect while wading in the surf or swimming just beyond the breakers; some of these also wash ashore. The abyssal range is the deep water below the continental slope—these shells are rarely accessable to us as beachgoers.

Go to the beach prepared with some plastic bags (quart- and gallon-sized food storage bags are good) and a few paper towels. I like to take a small backpack, which leaves my hands free and gives me a way to carry my shoes if I'm going to wade. I have found plenty of shells, and sea glass too, by searching at the water line as the tide begins to rise. (When crouching in this area, it's easy to get the seat of your pants soaked by the wave you don't see coming, so don't be surprised when it happens.)

Shells from this intertidal range are the easiest to gather. Be sure to check and see if the shells are inhabited. Quite often the owner will still be at home if you have picked up a shell from a tidal pool. Gently return it as close as possible to where you found it. Other times, the inhabitant may be present, but dead. In that case you will need to clean the shell.

If you have the time and want to keep the cleaning process very natural, you might want to use the "rotting" method. That's exactly what you let happen: you bury the shell in soft sand or soil and let the ants and other creepy-crawlies do their thing. Of course, this must be done away from the house and it will need to be checked from time to time to see if the process is complete.

A quicker and easier method is to put smelly shells into a half-and-half solution of bleach and water—which will also get rid of the remnants of anything else that may have grown on the outside of the shell. Use a soft brush and clean water to rinse them after the bleach bath. While this is effective—and for plain white shells it's perfect—I have found that it sometimes ruins brightly colored shells. For those, use white vinegar instead of bleach.

Once the shells are clean and dry, the fun of finding the right places for them begins. This may naturally be an ongoing process: as our energy interacts with the shell's energy—as we get to know each other—we find where it belongs. Just as with other things in our homes, we need to rearrange them from time to time to get the energy flowing, to stir the cauldron of life.

HEALTH: OURS AND THE OCEAN'S

Sea Bathing

Since ancient times the sea has been considered the *primum mobile*—the "first cause" of life, and our prime source of health. As more people became city dwellers, fresh air, sunshine, and seawater was a draw for those seeking to improve their health in nature. By the eighteenth century in Europe, the seaside resort was a destination, beckoning with the curative properties of sea bathing. One of the scientific reasons sea air is healthy is that its negatively charged ions (created by the action of the water) help "re-energize the whole system." In addition, the minerals in sea air that are absorbed by the lungs cleanse the tissue and help to "relieve inflammation caused by gritty metropolitan pollution."[19]

If you have the chance to visit the shore in summer—or as a winter break—you can create a powerful experience while swimming in the ocean. Go to the beach when there are few people to distract you, and first take time for a sea centering. When you have completed your centering, slowly walk toward the water. Keep your senses wide open so you can experience every nuance: the feel of sand against your feet, the sensation as you step into the water. Note these things, but don't stay too focused on any one element of the experience.

As you step in deeper, feel the pull of the current and the push of each wave. Walk in as far as you are comfortable and able to stand safely. Close your eyes and breathe deeply. Soak it in with all of your senses. Repeat your sea centering, letting your energy flow with the sea's rhythm. When you have completed a cycle, remain in the water a few more minutes. Observe the feel of the moving water and how your own rhythms might mesh with it. When you are ready, return to shore—or stay and swim.

If you don't have a chance to visit the beach, try a healing sea bath at home. Healing baths have been used since ancient times for emotional, physical, and spiritual well-being. For centuries, ritual baths held an important preparatory function. However, even though we may like to steal away for a nice long soak in the tub once in a while, we don't generally approach a bath as a healing or spiritual tool.

Just as preparing for meditation is important, so too is preparing for a special bath. You will need one or two pounds of sea salt for this. It goes without saying: make sure you have plenty of time and adequate privacy. To enhance the experience, use your ocean candles and an ocean-sound recording. Place some favorite seashells around the edge of the tub. Draw bath water that is warm enough to dissolve the sea salt, then

---

19 James Loehr and Jeffrey Migdow, *Breathe In Breathe Out*, 42–43.

adjust the temperature as needed. Fill the tub enough so you can immerse most of your body. Get in and notice how moving your arms back and forth slowly can create a sensation of gentle waves.

Lean back, relax, and do your sea centering. (You might try holding a shell over your heart or making the shell mudra with your hands.) Afterward, keep your eyes closed and enjoy the energy. When the water cools, end the bath or add a little warm water and continue to relax.

Even the simple act of bathing can strengthen our connection with the sea and, ultimately, the natural world.

Food from the Sea

The ocean has been a major source of food ever since humans first wandered to the beach and discovered the vast supply under the waves. Foods from the sea remain the basis of healthy Mediterranean and Asian diets. More recently, the omega-3 fatty acids of coldwater fish have been shown to reduce the risk of heart disease and help fight breast and colon cancers.[20] Salmon is usually the best choice for omega-3s but tuna, mackerel, whitefish, and herring are also good sources. (Some fish may contain toxins, however, so speak with your doctor before increasing your fish intake or changing your diet. Do some research—and see the notes on seafood under "When You Take, Don't Forget to Give" on page 163.)

What about sea salt? Throughout this book we have spoken of its cleansing and empowering qualities; it is the symbol of wisdom. Many consider sea salt a purer form than commercial table salts, which are mined from the earth and include additives such as aluminum compounds. While this may prevent the salt from caking, it may not be something you want to add to your diet. The iodine in most salts is not always recommended, either.[21] Again, you may want to check with your doctor before making any dietary changes.

---

20 Matthew Hoffman, *The Doctors Book of Food Remedies*, 212.

21 Andrew Weil, M.D., *Natural Health, Natural Medicine*, 60.

The ocean also teems with plant life. But our term "seaweed" unfortunately suggests all those undesirable plants that grow in our gardens or lawns. Perhaps a better phrase, as noted by Lauren Mukamal Camp, is "sea vegetable."[22] Sea veggies have been used medicinally for goiter and glandular diseases in China since 3000 BCE. The ancient Romans used them to treat burns and other skin wounds.[23] Today seaweed is commonly used in aspirin and antacids as well as other commercial products. In fact, there are some 20,000 known species of sea vegetables.[24]

But for Westerners, sea plants are mysterious and misunderstood. If you have not tasted them, I suggest going to a Japanese or vegetarian restaurant to sample them. Have you already enjoyed miso soup? It's not the tofu that makes it tasty, it's the kombu or wakame seaweed that gives it flavor. And do you know what is used to wrap sushi, vegetables, and rice? Yep, it's seaweed.

While we may not be able to buy fresh seaweed locally, dried sea vegetables are readily available at many health food stores. As for the nutritional buzzwords: seaweed is low in calories and cholesterol. And it may be a surprise that the sodium content in a serving is about the same as in a carrot.[25] Seaweed is also a great source of vitamins and minerals. If you try it at home you don't have to start with a huge plateful; begin slowly, mixing it with land-grown vegetables for starters. Most importantly, do what works for you.

And here's a final note on the topic of seafood and cooking: Scallop shells can be used for baking, and they make a wonderful presentation for individual portions of fish. Bake them in a conventional oven, and handle them carefully after removing them, as the shells retain heat rather well.

---

22 Lauren Mukamal Camp, "Savory Sea Veggies," *Yoga Journal,* 110.

23 Groves, *The Oceans,* 60.

24 Camp, "Savory Sea Veggies," 110.

25 Ibid.

When You Take, Don't Forget to Give

Today, one issue with seafood is the potential level of toxins that it may contain. Pollution continues to be a major problem, not just for our own health, but for the ocean's as well. Indeed, they are inextricably linked. But sadly, many people do not realize that it is not only an industrial pollution problem; many of the toxins causing the problem come from our homes. A huge quantity of household cleaning and gardening chemicals end up in the ocean. Regardless of where we live, we all have an impact on the ocean's health. Anything that gets into a stream, river, or lake eventually ends up in the sea.

We discard too much into the ocean, and we also take too much out of it. Overfishing has greatly depleted fish numbers worldwide. While affluent countries benefit from the global market, buying fish from anywhere in the world, developing nations are suffering the economic and nutritional impact.

We must personalize our environmental awareness and responsibility. But what can one person do? Contact your representatives in Congress about the United States' ocean policy. Be aware of any chemicals you use in your home and on your lawn; remember where they will end up. If we believe that the natural world is sacred, it makes no sense to destroy it.

Choose seafood wisely and stay educated. The Monterey Bay Aquarium in California offers a wealth of information about safeguarding sea life and making smart seafood choices: check the website (www.monterey bayaquarium.org). Its Seafood Watch Pocket Guides are easy to use and available for all regions of the United States. Voting with our wallets can send a powerful message. There are many other websites and other sources for information.

Don't worry: you don't have to become an environmental crusader in order to make a difference. Be aware and mindful and make conscious decisions about how you live in this world. Your energy will have an effect. As we live our lives in mindfulness, our intentions ripple out, joining those of other like-minded people, creating a tide of positive energy that touches everyone and everything.

As you continue to explore Sea Magic, remember to give back. Keep the sacred rhythms of the ocean through your sea centerings and meditations, and then open your heart: send love and energy to Mother Ocean. Receive healing energy and return healing energy.

JOURNAL QUESTIONS

1. What do you feel when you stand in the light of the full moon?

2. How has the cosmic sea centering expanded your personal energy?

3. What awareness has the shell mudra brought to you?

4. What changes are taking place in your life that you can attribute to working with the ocean's energy?

$\mathscr{I}$N CONCLUSION

EBB AND FLOW

We live on the big blue marble: the water planet. We are physically and physiologically connected with the sea. It is our lifeblood, and for millennia the ocean has fed us and nurtured us. We are drawn to the sea, mesmerized by its beauty and hypnotic rhythm. We respond to its primal call, whether we are near or far from the coast.

Our emotions are associated with the element of water, so working with sea energy can lead us deep into this area of the psyche. With the sea centering practice, we connect with our inner ocean and find the strength to plumb the depths of our feelings. We also gain a grounded yet fluid stability that helps us cope with our busy and often frantic world. With the power of the ocean supporting us, we can create the physical and mental space we need to define and follow our inner path. I don't believe that we were put on this earth to worry about what is happening on Wall Street or next door at the proverbial Jones household. Dr. Wayne Dyer said that "connecting to intention means listening to your heart and conducting yourself based on what your inner voice tells you is your purpose here."[1]

When we develop a true inner path, we can live in wonder and appreciation of each day. The sacred and the secular parts of our lives

---

1 Dyer, *Power of Intention*, 86.

intertwine. "Each day is a secret story woven around the radiant heart of wonder," in the words of John O'Donohue.[2] To feel deep within our souls the beauty of a sunset or a wave lapping the shore, to feel the pull of the moon and the sway of the tides, is to find our place in the greater cosmos. The sea has a way of getting us to slow down and reflect on the things that are important on a soul level.

From an early age we are barraged with messages that we must compete, achieve, and constantly do things. But we are often left with little time for self-exploration. If we don't know who we are, how do we know what we want to do, what to compete for, what to achieve? By working with sea energy we can fine-tune our intuition so we know when to float and observe or take action and swim. If we don't know how to take soul nourishment, our inner self will wither away.

By using sea centerings, ocean breath, and other techniques we can discern and follow our own energetic ebb and flow. We can discover that we have the ability to nourish our souls and even transform our lives. A sea change merges our inner and outer selves, and we feel we can fully inhabit the person we were meant to be. We can live with an attitude of gratitude. When we see our life for the tremendous gift that it is, we can touch the magic and mystery of the natural world and know that we are part of it. We see that we are embodied spirits with the chance to learn about our true nature while we are alive in nature.

With an altar, we can demarcate a special place that our intention and energy transforms into a space that transcends our everyday experience. It becomes a safe space where we open our hearts and psyches. Our altars become tools for gnosis—knowledge that comes from spiritual insight and self-illumination. Like the ebb and flow of tides, a sea altar can evolve over time and reflect what we hold in our hearts and minds.

We can enhance our altar space by creating a sea circle of energy to further manifest our intention and connection with the ocean. With no beginning or end, our sea circle is a perpetual tidal flow where we share in the mysteries of the turning and returning cycles and of time and

---

2 O'Donohue, *Eternal Echoes*, 77.

eternity. And as we move deeper into self, we look for our totem animal in the form of a sea fetch—a marine creature that offers itself to serve as our special guide. Our fetch helps bring information to the surface where it can enter our awareness. Our fetch may symbolize who we are, or it may represent the qualities that we wish to foster in ourselves.

The ocean is a netherworld between reality and myth. The ocean's mystery and greatness has enticed people to seek in its endless rolling rhythms an explanation for the essential questions of life. The very ocean itself seems alive, and through the human imagination it has given rise to mythological deities and creatures over the ages. As fantastic as these legends may be, they have brought order and understanding into the lives of seekers through the millennia. As we have seen, sea deities and saints helped our ancestors make sense of nature. With human faces, as well as many human foibles, they can still teach us that there is more to this world than what we thought possible. They help us explore the misty horizons and connect with the ocean's vast power.

Like the sea itself, sea deities were often portrayed as beautiful and almost always as mysterious. Some were helpful to humankind and some downright treacherous. Some saints, too, found adventure on the sea and many, including Mother Mary, worked with Mother Ocean in aid of people. Celtic, Egyptian, Greek, Sumerian and other peoples believed in a land of spirit, of the dead, of the ancestors—a land that lay just beyond the horizon or hidden under the sea. The magical Otherworld was a place of peace and beauty. It was an eternal paradise in which to rest as well as a place of rebirth and transformation. Whether an Otherworld of spirit, a place of passage, or a breathtaking paradise, these realms serve to teach us that there is more to this world than meets the eye.

Just as mythical deities were used by ancient people to explain the wondrous powers of the ocean, sea creatures have their place in legends worldwide. Some were meant to scare and warn, while others provided comfort or gave credence to the hidden realms.

As the wise sages of antiquity knew, this mythological legacy can help us learn the larger lessons of life. The ocean has always been a part of this legacy, because we humans continually seek the places where we belong.

Still, as much as we feel we are at home with the sea, we lack the ability to control it. The ocean keeps us on our edge and teaches us to fine-tune our senses. No matter how well we know the sea, it will always surprise us and teach new lessons.

Creation stories from around the globe have said what science eventually showed: that life began in the sea. That primeval ocean nurtured the chemical compounds that are the building blocks of life. Likewise, the mighty ocean may have wiped the slate clean and allowed a new beginning. Mother Ocean created and recreated life. Creatures may have crawled or wriggled their way out of the sea in the far distant past, but later, Mother Ocean was there with open arms to receive some of their mammalian descendants back into the watery fold.

Mother Ocean still offers us gifts continually, washing her wonders ashore for our delight. Seashells are gifts that offer a tantalizing promise of discovery about ourselves as well as about the sea. Their energy and beauty attract us; their shapes and color patterns suggest flowing movement that echoes the mystery and rhythm of their watery home. The simplicity of a seashell holds incredible energy that can guide us on our journey. From the womb of Mother Ocean, seashells bring us beauty, balance, and luminosity. Each type of shell has its unique energy and associations that aid and support us as we wade into the waters of our inner journey. We can call on the power of shells at any time with the seashell mudra. Holding our hands in the shape of a conch summons the essence of sea energy to calm and empower us.

In most instances seashells are wonderful gifts from the sea, but at other times they can carry oracular messages. The meaning of these messages may not be clear immediately, but when we open our hearts we can welcome the knowledge we are meant to receive. Through seashell divination we call on Mother Ocean's power to help unite the personal with the mystical by bringing our innermost issues into the light where they can be examined and addressed. With mindfulness and truth, seashell divination becomes a tool for self-exploration that also serves to strengthen our intuitive abilities.

We can also enhance our intuition by connecting with the moon. Among the sea's many fascinations is its interplay with the sun and moon. Circular tides of energy move continually through the heavens, the sea, and our own bodies, connecting us with the universe. We come to realize that we are children of the cosmos and the cosmic sea. From the rhythm of our inner sea we connect with all that is. Just as the tides and moon wax and wane, so does our personal energy ebb and flow. Tuning into these patterns brings us to a new level of awareness and insight.

As we tune into ourselves and the world around us, we find that our own health and the health of the environment are inextricably linked. Food from the sea—animal or plant—can be a nutritional powerhouse; however, we must take carefully and leave enough to maintain healthy ecosystems. This is not difficult; it only requires us to be aware and mindful of how we live. Just as a boat's wake is a temporary wave on the water, so too should our time on this earth leave little impact on the natural world.

We are continually drawn by mystery because we are seekers. We want to find out who we are, what we are, and where we belong. There is a deep part of us that needs to search for answers, that longs for connection.

We live on the big blue marble: the water planet. We are children of the sea. When we stand on the shore and gaze at Mother Ocean, our hearts open with awe. We feel alive and connected, and we know that we are more than our physical bodies. The purity and power of the ocean gives us the clarity to see and understand our journey. The salt of wisdom comes down to us through the ages. Embraced by the circle of the sea, we can find the hidden land, the paradise that exists within our souls.

Tenet mare sal sapientia: the sea holds the salt of wisdom.

*A*PPENDIX A

MIND MAPPING

The technique called mind mapping was invented by Tony Buzan as a tool to free the mind's hidden power. It's a nonlinear brainstorming technique that calls on our powers of association. Mind mapping has been used as an alternative to the hierarchical outline approach to organizing concepts and ideas. It is also used for problem solving and inspiring creativity. Every human mind associates things differently, and as a result every mind map is unique.

I have found this technique to be a valuable aid for journaling about emotions. After meditation or especially after a sea journey, creating a mind map is a way to delve into our inner worlds and get some details down on paper quickly. Later, you can refer back to it and write more completely about your experience.

Start by thinking of a keyword or short phrase for a "seed idea" or question. Write it in the middle of a sheet of paper and draw a circle around it. Then write down the next word that you associate with that seed idea, circle it and connect it with a line to the seed keyword. Now write a keyword for the next thought, circle it, and draw a line to whichever thought triggered it (or it might be both). Keep going and soon you have a network of circles and lines that may resemble a spider's web. I like to think of these as bubbles—thoughts and information bubbling up from the inner self.

In this map, *earth* was the seed keyword. A number of various concepts emerged as I let my mind flow from one connection to another. Try it with the word *ocean* and see how many bubbles rise to the surface.

Then try it in a journaling session when you are working with your feelings. It may not be appropriate for every time you write in your journal, but you may find that it is a useful tool and develop your own ways of working with it.

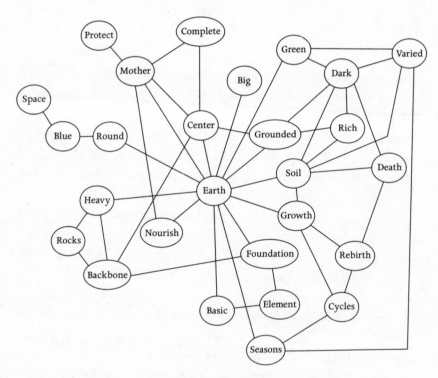

A sample mind map beginning with the keyword "earth."

$\mathcal{A}$PPENDIX B

RUNES AND OGHAM

THE RUNES

Developed in the first or second century, the runes are an alphabet used in northern Europe, the British Isles, and Iceland for communications as well as magic and divination.

Rune Character	Letters	Name(s)	Basic Associations
ᚠ	F	Fehu, Feoh	Riches, possessions, accumulated wealth
ᚢ	U	Ur, Uruz	Physical and mental strength, good health
ᚦ	Th/P	Thorn, Thurisaz	Issues, work to be done
ᚱ	R	Rad, Radio	Travel, progress
ᚨ	A	As, Ansuz	Answers, signals and signs
ᚲ	K	Ken, Kenaz	Creativity, inspiration, enlightenment
ᚷ	G	Gyfu, Gebo	Partnership, relationships

Continued on next page

The Runes (continued)

Rune Character	Letters	Name(s)	Basic Associations
ᚹ	W	Wunjo, Wyn	Joy, happiness, peace with self
ᚺ	H	Hagal, Hagalaz	Disruption, change
ᚾ	N	Nyd, Nauthiz	Constraint, self-imposed obstacles
ᛁ	I	Is, Isa	Active stillness
ᛃ	J	Jera, Ger	Reaping, beneficial outcomes
ᛇ	E/EI	Eoh, Eihwaz	Trust, reliability
ᛈ	P	Peorth, Perth	Decisions, inner transformation
ᛉ	Z	Elhaz, Algiz	Protection
ᛋ	S	Sigel, Sowelu	Wholeness
ᛏ	T	Tyr, Teiwaz	Justice, victory
ᛒ	B	Beorc, Berkana	Growth, new beginnings
ᛗ	M	Man, Mannaz	Self
ᛞ	D	Dagaz, Daeg	Completion, end of a cycle
ᛟ	O	Odal, Othila	Reflection
ᛜ	NG	Ing, Inguz	Successful conclusion
ᛚ	L	Lagu, Laguz	Emotional balance, relationships, the sea and the unending depths of the ocean

THE OGHAM TREE ALPHABET

The Ogham originated between 300 and 600 CE and was used by Celtic people for brief inscriptions and magi. It may have also been used as a teaching tool or *aide-mémoire* by Bardic poets.

Ogham Character	Letters	Names	Associated Tree(s)	Basic Associations
T	B	**Beith**, Beth	Birch	Beginnings, release, renewal, change
TT	L	**Luis**	Rowan	Quickening, insight, dedication, expression, blessings
TTT	F, V	**Fearn**, Fern	Alder	Foundation, guardian, evolving spirit
TTTT	S	**Saille**, Saile,	Willow	Intuition, flexibility, knowledge, relationships
TTTTT	N	**Nion**, Nuin	Ash	Transitions, connections, creativity
⊥	H	**Huath**, Uath	Hawthorn	Protection/defense, hope, healing, spiritual energies
⊥⊥	D	**Duir**, Dair	Oak	Strength, self-confidence, justice
⊥⊥⊥	T	**Tinne**, Teine	Holly	Hearth and home, unity, protection, courage, guidance
⊥⊥⊥⊥	C, K	**Coll**, Call	Hazel	Wisdom, knowledge of secrets, creativity
⊥⊥⊥⊥⊥	Q, CC	**Quert**, Ceirt	Apple	Eternity, love, faithfulness, rebirth
⫻	M	**Muin**	Vine Bramble	Inward journeys, lifting confusion, opening, learning lessons
⫻⫻	G	**Gort**	Ivy	Growth, wildness, development, confronting the mystical

Continued on next page

The Ogham Tree Alphabet (continued)

Ogham Character	Letters	Names	Associated Tree(s)	Basic Associations
⁗	Ng	**Ngetal**, nGétal	Reed	Health and healing, adaptation, gathering
⁗	St, Z, SS	**Straif**, Straith	Blackthorn	Authority, control, strength in adversity
⁗	R	**Ruis**	Elder	Maturity, abundance, awareness, transition
+	A	**Ailm**, Ailim	Fir, Pine	Perspective, reaching, rising above
⧺	O	**Onn**, Ohn	Gorse	Hope, persistence
⧻	U, W	**Ur**, Ura	Heather	Passion, generosity
⧻	E	**Eadhadh**, Eadha	Aspen	Endurance, communication, courage, success
⧻	I, J, Y	**Iodho**, Iod-hadh	Yew	Death, transition, endings
✕	EA, CH, K	**Éabhadh**, Ebad	Honeysuckle, Aspen	Attracting sweetness of life
◇	OI, TH	**Oir**, Or	Spindletree, Ivy	Creativity, inspiration
ᚏ	UI, PE	**Uilleann**, Uilen	Beech, Honeysuckle	Manifesting intentions
✕	IO, PH	**Ifin**, Iphin	Gooseberry, Beech	Clarity of vision, second sight
▦	AE, X, XI	**Amhancholl**, Mór	Witch Hazel, Pine; also associated with the Sea	Cleansing, purifying, releasing

$\mathscr{B}$IBLIOGRAPHY

Abbott, R. Tucker, Ph.D. *Kingdom of the Seashell*. New York: Crown Publishers, Inc., 1979.

————. *Shells*. New York, NY: Portland House, 1989.

———— and Morris, Percy A. *Shells of the Atlantic & Gulf Coasts & the West Indies*. New York, NY: Houghton Mifflin Company, 1995.

Alexander, Hartley Burr. *North American Mythology*. Norwood, MA: The Plimpton Press, 1937.

Amussen, Susan D., and Adele F. Seeff (editors). *Attending to Early Modern Women*. Cranbury, NJ: Associated University Presses, Inc., 1998.

Andrews, Ted. *Animal Speak: Magical Powers of Creatures Great and Small*. St. Paul, MN: Llewellyn Worldwide, 1993.

Asala, Joanne. *Celtic Folklore Cooking*. St. Paul, MN: Llewellyn Publications, 2004.

Aston, William G. *A History of Japanese Literature*. Safety Harbor, FL: Simon Publications, 2001.

Baggott, Andy. *Celtic Wisdom*. London: Piatkus Publishers Ltd., 1999.

Bassett, Fletcher S. *Legends and Superstitions of the Sea and of Sailors*. Detroit: Singing Tree Press, 1971.

Baur, Brian S. *The Sacred Landscape of the Inca: The Cusco Ceque System*. Austin, TX: The University of Texas Press, 1998.

Bayley, Harold. *Archaic England*. London: Chapman & Hall, Ltd., 1919.

Beck, Horace. *Folklore and the Sea*. Middletown, CT: Wesleyan University Press, 1973.

Bell, John. *Bell's New Pantheon or Historial Dictionary of the Gods, Demi Gods, Heroes and Fabulous Personages of Antiquity*. Whitefish, MT: Kessinger Publishing, 2003.

Bellows, Henry Adams (translator). *The Poetic Edda: The Mythological Poems*. Mineola, NY: Dover Publications, Inc., 2004.

Berrill, N.J., and Jacquelyn Berrill. *1001 Questions Answered About the Seashore*. New York: Dover Publishers, 1976.

Blum, Ralph. *The Book of Runes: A Handbook for the Use of an Ancient Oracle*. London: Headline Publishing PLC, 1993.

Blumetti, Robert. *The Book of Balder Rising*. Lincoln, NE: iUniverse, Inc., 2004.

Buzan, Tony, and Barry Buzan. *The Mind Map Book*. New York: E. P. Dutton, 1994.

Camp, Lauren Mukamal. "Savory Sea Veggies," *Yoga Journal*, March/April, 1998.

Carmichael, Alexander (translator). *Carmina Gadelica*. Edinburgh: Constable, 1900.

Carson, Rachel L., *The Edge of the Sea*. New York: Mariner Books, 1998.

———. *The Sea Around Us*. New York: Mentor Books, 1954.

Cashford, Jules. *The Moon: Myth and Image*. New York: Four Walls Eight Windows, 2002.

Chamberlain, Alexander F. *The Child and Childhood in Folk Thought*. Whitefish, MT: Kessinger Publishing, 2005.

Chocron, Daya Sarai. *The Healing Power of Seashells*. Findhorn, Scotland: Earthdancer Books, 2005.

Collings, Andrew. *Gateway to Atlantis: The Search for the Source of a Lost Civilization*. New York: Carroll & Graf Publishers, 2002.

Conway, D.J. *Little Book of Healing Magic*. Berkeley, CA: The Crossing Press, 2002.

———. *Moon Magic*. St. Paul, MN: Llewellyn Publications, 2003.

———. *Norse Magic*. St. Paul, MN: Llewellyn Publications, 2003.

Cooper, Patrinella. *Gypsy Magic: A Romany Book of Spells, Charms, and Fortune-Telling*. Boston: Weiser Books, 2002.

Cotterell, Arthur, and Rachel Storm. *The Ultimate Encyclopedia of Mythology*. New York: Hermes House, 1999.

Cunningham, Nancy Brady. *A Book of Women's Altars: Crate Sacred Spaces for Art, Worship, Solace, Celebrations*. Boston: Red Wheel, 2002.

Cunningham, Scott. *Cunningham's Encyclopedia of Crystal, Gem and Metal Magic*. St. Paul, MN: Llewellyn Publications, 2001.

———. *Earth, Air, Fire & Water: More Techniques of Natural Magic*. Woodbury, MN: Llewellyn Publications, 2005.

——— and Harrington, David. *Spell Crafts: Creating Magical Objects*. St. Paul, MN: Llewellyn Publications, 2003.

Cutts, Rev. E. L. *Scenes and Characters of the Middle Ages*. London: Virtue & Company, 1886.

Dance, S. Peter. *Shells*. New York: Dorling Kindersley, Inc., 1992.

Dietrich, Thomas. *The Origin of Culture and Civilization*. Austin, TX: Turnkey Press, 2005.

Douglass, Jackie Leatherbury, and Roger Tory Peterson. *Peterson First Guide to Shells of North America*. New York: Houghton Mifflin Company, 1989.

Dupuis, Elaine. *New Era for Eve: Myth and History Before Eve . . . and After*. Philadelphia: Xlibris Corporation, 2000.

Dyer, Wayne W. *The Power of Intention: Learning to Co-create Your World Your Way*. Carlsbad, CA: Hay House, Inc., 2004.

Eason, Cassandra. *A Complete Guide to Magic and Ritual: Using the Energy of Nature to Heal Your Life*. Freedom, CA: The Crossing Press, Inc., 2001.

———. *A Complete Guide to Night Magic*. New York: Citadel Press, 2003.

Eckel, Malcolm David. *Buddhism: Origins, Beliefs, Practices, Holy Texts, Sacred Places*. New York: Oxford University Press, 2002.

Ferguson, Diana. *The Magickal Year: A Pagan Perspective on the Natural World*. New York: Labyrinth Books, 1996.

Forty, Jo. *Mythology: A Visual Encyclopedia*. New York: Sterling Publishing Company, Inc., 2001.

Franklin, Anna. *The Celtic Animal Oracle*. London, England: Vega Books, 2003.

———. *The Illustrated Encyclopedia of Fairies*. London: Vega Books, 2002.

Fries, Jan. *Cauldron of the Gods: A Manual of Celtic Magic*. Oxford, England: Mandrake of Oxford, 2003.

Gaertner, Brigitte. Grimm, Christine M. (trans.). *Powerful Feng Shui Balancing Tools*. Twin Lakes, WI: Lotus Press, 2001.

Garrison, Tom. *Oceanography: An Invitation to Marine Science*. Belmont, CA: Brooks-Cole Publishing Company, 2001.

Gayley, Charles Mills. *The Classic Myths in English Literature*. Boston: Ginn & Company, 1903.

Gendler, J. Ruth (editor). *Changing Light: The Eternal Cycle of Night and Day*. New York: HarperCollins Publishers, 1991.

Gibson, Clare. *Goddess Symbols: Universal Signs of the Divine Female.* New York: Barnes & Noble Books, 1998.

Gimbutas, Marija. *The Civilization of the Goddess: The World of Old Europe.* San Francisco: HarperSanFrancisco, 1991.

Goddard, David. *The Sacred Magic of Angels.* Boston: Weiser, 1996.

Gonzaga, Shireen, and Marc Airhart. *Seashells.* Austin, TX: Earth and Sky Radio Series, August 2000.

González-Wippler, Migene. *The Complete Book of Spells, Ceremonies and Magic.* St. Paul, MN: Llewellyn Publications, 1988.

———. *Introduction to Seashell Divination.* New York: Original Publications, 1985.

———. *Santeria: The Religion.* St. Paul, MN: Llewellyn Publications, 2004.

Gosner, Kenneth L. *A Field Guide to the Atlantic Seashore.* Boston: Houghton Mifflin Co., 1979.

Greene, Rosalyn. *The Magic of Shapeshifting.* Boston: Weiser, 2000.

Greer, John Michael. *The New Encyclopedia of the Occult.* St. Paul, MN: Llewellyn Publications, 2004.

Grimal, Pierre. *The Dictionary of Classical Mythology.* Malden, MA: Blackwell Publishing, Ltd., 1996.

Groves, Don. *The Oceans: A Book of Questions and Answers.* New York: John Wiley & Sons, Inc., 1989.

Hanson, Michelle. *Ocean Oracle: What Seashells Reveal About Our True Nature.* Hillsboro, OR: Beyond Words Publishing, Inc., 2004.

Hard, Robin. *The Routledge Handbook of Greek Mythology.* New York: Routledge Taylor & Francis Group, 2004.

Harris, Eleanor L. *Ancient Egyptian Divination and Magic.* Boston: Weiser Books, 1998.

Hemenway, Priya. *Hindu Gods: The Spirit of the Divine*. San Francisco: Chronicle Books, 2003.

Herbermann, Charles G. (editor). *The Catholic Encyclopedia*. New York: The Encyclopedia Press, Inc., 1913.

Herbst, Philip H. *Wimmin Wimps & Wallflowers*. Yarmouth, ME: Intercultural Press Inc., 2001.

Herskovits, Melville J., and Frances S. Herskovits. *Dahomean Narrative: A Cross-Cultural Analysis*. Evanston, IL: Northwestern University Press, 1998.

Hinton, Sam. *Seashore Life of Southern California*. Berkeley: University of California Press, 1987.

Hirschi, Gertrud. *Mudras: Yoga in Your Hands*. Boston: Weiser Books, 2000.

Hoffman, Matthew (editor). *The Doctors Book of Food Remedies*. Emmaus, PA: Rodale Inc. 1998.

Howey, M. Oldfield. *The Horse in Magic and Myth*. Mineola, NY: Dover Publications, Inc., 2002.

Hubbell, Sue. *Waiting for Aphrodite: Journeys into the Time Before Bones*. New York: Mariner Books, 2000.

Hughes, Merritt Y., and A. S. P. Woodhouse. *A Variorum Commentary on the Poems of John Milton*. New York: Columbia University Press, 1972.

Hull, Clifford A., Steven R. Perkins, and Tracy Barr. *Latin for Dummies*. New York: Hungry Minds, Inc., 2002.

Hulse, David Allen. *The Western Mysteries—An Encyclopedic Guide to the Sacred Languages & Magickal Systems of the World*. St. Paul, MN: Llewellyn Publications, 2000.

Husain, Shahrukh. *The Goddess: Power, Sexuality and the Feminine Divine*. Ann Arbor, MI: University of Michigan Press, 2003.

Illes, Judika. *Emergency Magic: 150 Spells for Surviving the Worst-Case Scenario*. Gloucester, MA: Fair Winds Press, 2002.

Jacobsen, Thorkild. *Treasures of Darkness: A History of Mesopotamian Religion*. New Haven: Yale University Press, 1976.

Jacobson, Morris K., and William K. Emerson. *Shells from Cape Cod to Cape May with Special Reference to the New York City Area*. New York: Dover Publications, Inc., 1971.

Jobes, Gertrude. *Dictionary of Mythology Folklore and Symbols*. New York: The Scarecrow Press, Inc., 1962.

Johns, Veronica Parker. *She Sells Seashells*. New York: Funk & Wagnalls, 1968.

Jung, C. G. *Mysterium Coniunctionis: An Inquiry into the Separation and Synthesis of Psychic Opposites in Alchemy*. Princeton, NJ: Princeton University Press, 1976.

Kaplan, Eugene H. *A Field Guide to Southeastern and Caribbean Seashores: Cape Hatteras to the Gulf Coast*. New York: Houghton Mifflin Company, 1988.

Knight, Brenda. *Gem Magic: Crystals and Gemstones for Love, Luck and Power*. Gloucester, MA: Fair Winds Press, 2004.

Knight, Sirona. *The Little Giant Encyclopedia of Runes*. New York: Sterling Publishing Company, Inc. 2000.

Kodratoff, Yves. *Nordic Magic Healing*. Boca Raton, FL: Universal Publishers, 2003.

Kunz, George Frederick. *The Magic of Jewels and Charms*. Mineola, NY: Dover Publications, Inc. 1997.

Kynes, Sandra. *A Year of Ritual: Sabbats & Esbats for Solitaries & Covens*. St. Paul, MN: Llewellyn Publications, 2002.

———. *Whispers from the Woods: The Lore & Magic of Trees*. Woodbury, MN: Llewellyn Publications, 2006.

Lee, Guy Carleton (editor-in-chief). *The World's Orators*. New York: G. P. Putnam's Sons, 1900.

Lenormant, François. *Chaldean Magic: Its Origin and Development*. Boston: Weiser Books, 1999.

Lindbergh, Anne Morrow. *Gift from the Sea*. New York: Pantheon Books, 1975.

Lloyd, Ellen. *Voices from Legendary Times*. Lincoln, NE: iUniverse, 2005.

Loehr, James E., Ed.D., and Jeffrey A. Migdow, M.D. *Breathe In Breathe Out: Inhale Energy and Exhale Stress by Guiding and Controlling Your Breathing*. Alexandria, VA: Time Life Books, 1999.

MacEowen, Frank. *The Mist-Filled Path: Celtic Wisdom for Exiles, Wanderers, and Seekers*. Novato, CA: New World Library, 2002.

MacKillop, James. *Oxford Dictionary of Celtic Mythology*. Oxford, England: Oxford University Press, 1998.

MacGregor, Trish and Germondo, Millie. *Animal Totems: Power and Prophecy of Your Animal Guides*. Gloucester, MA: Fair Winds Press, 2004.

Markale, Jean. *The Celts*. Rochester, VT: Inner Traditions, 1993.

Marshall, Marlene Hurley. *Shell Chic: The Ultimate Guide to Decorating Your Home with Seashells*. North Adams, MA: Storey Books, 2002.

Matthews, Caitlin. *Mabon and the Guardians of Celtic Britain: Hero Myths in the Mabinogion*. Rochester, VT: Inner Traditions, 2002.

———, and John Matthews. *The Encyclopedia of Celtic Wisdom: The Celtic Shaman's Sourcebook*. Rockport, MA: Element Books, Inc., 1994.

McClatchy, J. D. (editor). *Poems of the Sea*. New York: Alfred A. Knopf, 2001.

McKinley, Robin, and Peter Dickinson. *Water: Tales of Elemental Spirits*. New York: G. P. Putnam's Sons, 2002.

Meinkoth, Norman A. *National Audubon Society's Field Guide to North American Seashore Creatures*. New York: Alfred A. Knopf, Inc., 2002.

Michaels, Lisa. *The Elemental Forces of Creation Oracle*. Lilburn, GA: The Institute of Conscious Expression, 2005.

Milton, John. *Comus*. New York: Maynard, Merrill and Company, 1898.

Misra, Neelesh, and Rupak Sanyal. *Ancient Tribe Survives Tsunami*. Jirkatang, India: Associated Press, January 6, 2005, www.cbsnews.com/stories/2005/01/04/world/main664729.shtml.

Morningstar, Sally. *Love Magic: Potions, Rituals & Spells to Enchant a Lover Into Your Life*. New York: Sterling Publishing Company, Inc., 2000.

Morrison, Dorothy. *Everyday Moon Magic*. St. Paul, MN: Llewellyn Publications, 2004.

Mountainwater, Shekhinah. *Ariadne's Thread: A Workbook of Goddess Magic*. Freedom, CA: The Crossing Press, 1991.

Nicholson, John. *Animal Architects*. Crows Nest, NSW, Australia: Allen & Unwin, 2003.

O'Donohue, John. *Anam Cara: A Book of Celtic Wisdom*. New York: Cliff Street Books, 1997.

———. *Eternal Echoes: Celtic Reflections on Our Yearning to Belong*. New York: Cliff Street Books, 1999.

O'Dubhain, Searles. *The Knowledge of the Trees*. Smyra, GA: *Keltria Journal*, Issue 31, The Henge of Keltria, 1996.

Ohara, Rei, and Akemi Hotta. *Mantee*. San Francisco: Chronicle Books, 1998.

Oliver, Jeanne and Roddis Miles. *Brittany and Normandy*. Oakland, CA: Lonely Planet Publications, 2004.

Pagels, Elaine. *The Gnostic Gospels*. New York: Random House, 1979.

Perry, Richard. *The Polar Worlds*. New York: Taplinger Publishing Co., Inc., 1973.

Perry, W. J. *The Origin of Magic and Religion*. Whitefish, MT: Kessinger Publishing, 2003.

Pigott, Grenville, and Adam Gottlob Oehlenschläger. *A Manual of Scandinavian Mythology*. New York: Arno Press, 1978.

Pilkey, Orrin, Tracy Monegan Rice, and William J. Neal. *How to Read a North Carolina Beach*. Chapel Hill, NC: The University of North Carolina Press, 2004.

Pinches, Theophilus G. *The Religion of Babylonia and Assyria*. Whitefish, MT: Kessinger Publishing, 2004.

Proctor, Noble S., and Patrick J. Lynch. *A Field Guide to North Atlantic Wildlife: Marine Mammals, Seabirds, Fish and Other Sea Life*. New Haven: Yale University Press, 2005.

Pule, John. "Ocean Song to Myself," in *Whetu Moana: Contemporary Polynesian Poems in English* edited by Albert Wendt, Reina Whaitire, and Robert Sullivan. Honolulu: University of Hawaii Press, 2003.

Ralston, W. R. S. *Songs of the Russian People as Illustrative of Slavonic Mythology and Russian Social Life*. Whitefish, MT: Kessinger Publishing, 2004.

Regardie, Israel. *The Golden Dawn: A Complete Course in Practical Ceremonial Magic*. St. Paul, MN: Llewellyn Publications, 2003.

Renée, Janina. *By Candlelight: Rites for Celebration, Blessing & Prayer*. St. Paul, MN: Llewellyn Publications, 2004.

Richardson, Sandra Cheryl. *Magickal Formularia: A Study in Formulary Magick*. Miami, FL: White Starr Publishing, 2004.

Rolleston, T. W. *Celtic Myths and Legends*. New York: Dover Publications, Inc., 1990.

Rose, Carol. *Giants, Monsters and Dragons: An Encyclopedia of Folklore, Legend and Myth*. New York: W. W. Norton & Company, Inc., 2000.

Ross, David A. *The Fisherman's Ocean*. Mechanicsburg, PA: Stackpole Books, 2000.

Rydberg, Viktor. *Teutonic Mythology*. Whitefish, MT: Kessinger Publishing, 2004.

Sabelli, Bruno. *Simon & Schuster's Guide to Shells*. New York: Simon & Schuster Inc., 1979.

Salzberg, Sharon. *Faith: Trusting Your own Deepest Experience*. New York: Riverhead Books, 2002.

Sawyer, Peter H. *Kings and Vikings: Scandinavia and Europe AD 700–1100*. New York: Routledge, 2000.

Schutz, Bernard F. *Gravity from the Ground Up*. Cambridge: Cambridge University Press, 2003.

Seely, John B. *The Wonders of Elora*. London: G. B. Whittaker, 1825.

Seiss, Joseph A. *The Gospel in the Stars*. Grand Rapids, MI: Kregel Publications, 1972.

Seyffert, Oskar, Dr. *A Dictionary of Classical Antiquities, Mythology, Religion, Literature and Art*. Whitefish, MT: Kessinger Publishing, 2006.

Skafte, Dianne, Ph.D. *Listening to the Oracle: The Ancient Art of Finding Guidance in the Signs and Symbols All Around Us*. New York: HarperSanFrancisco, 1997.

Southey, Robert. *The Poetical Works of Robert Southey*. London: Longman, Orme, Brown, Green & Longmans, 1838.

Soyer, Alexis. *Food, Cookery and Dining in Ancient Times*. Mineola, NY: Dover Publications, Inc., 2004.

Spence, Lewis. *The History of Atlantis*. Whitefish, MT: Kessinger Publishing, 2003.

———. *The Magic Arts in Celtic Britain*. Mineola, NY: Dover Publications, Inc., 1999.

———. *The Minor Traditions of British Mythology*. New York: Arno Press, 1979.

Starhawk. Spiral Dance: *A Rebirth of the Ancient Religion of the Great Goddess*. San Francisco: HarperSanFrancisco, 1989.

Stewart, R. J. *The Living World of Faery*. Glastonbury, England: Gothic Image Publications, 1995.

Sykes, Egerton. *Everyman's Dictionary of Non-Classical Mythology*. New York: E.P. Dutton & Company, Inc., 1965.

Taylor, Dave. *Florida Manatees*. Calgary, Alberta, Canada: Weigl Educational Publishers, 2003.

Telesco, Patricia. *A Kitchen Witch's Cookbook*. St. Paul, MN: Llewellyn Publications, 2004.

———. *365 Goddess: A Daily Guide to the Magic and Inspiration of the Goddess*. San Francisco: HarperSanFrancisco, 1998.

Thomas, William, and Kate Pavitt. *The Book of Talismans, Amulets and Zodiacal Gems*. Whitefish, MT: Kessinger Publishing, 1994.

Thompson, Gerry Maguire. *Celtic Oracle: How to Foretell the Future Using Ancient Folklore*. Edison, NJ: Chartwell Books, Inc. 1999.

Tigunait, Pandit Rajmani. *Inner Quest: Yoga's Answers to Life's Questions*. Honesdale, PA: Himalayan Institute Press, 2002.

———. *The Yoga Sutras*. Honesdale, PA: *Yoga International* magazine, January/February, 2006.

Tolle, Eckhart. *The Power of Now: A Guide to Spiritual Enlightenment*. Novato, CA: New World Library, 1999.

Topping, Margaret. *Proust's Gods*. New York: Oxford University Press, 2000.

Toulson, Shirley. *The Celtic Year: A Celebration of Celtic Christian Saints, Sites and Festivals*. London: Vega, 2002.

Van den Berk, M. F. M. *The Magic Flute: Die Zauber Flöte: An Alchemical Allegory*. Boston: Brill, 2004.

Vanhaeren, Marian, Francesco d'Errico, Chris Stringer, Sarah L. James, Jonathan A. Todd, Henk K. Mienis. *Middle Paleolithic Shell Beads in Israel and Algeria.* Washington, DC: Science/AAAS, *Science,* vol. 312, no. 5781, June 23, 2006.

Voeks, Robert A. *Sacred Leaves of Candomble: African Magic, Medicine, and Religion in Brazil.* Austin, TX: University of Texas Press, 1997.

Ward, Kennan. *Journeys with the Ice Bear.* Minocqua, WI: NorthWord Press, Inc. 1996.

Ward, Nathalie. *Stellwagen Bank: A Guide to the Whales, Seabirds and marine Life of the Stellwagen Bank National Marine Sanctuary.* Camden, ME: Down East Books, 1995.

Weatherstone, Lunaea. *Celtic Mandala Journal.* Berkeley: Amber Lotus Publishing, 2003.

Weil, Andrew, M.D. *Natural Health, Natural Medicine: A Comprehensive Manual for Wellness and Self-care.* New York: Houghton Mifflin Company, 1998.

Wilk, Harry. White, John Sampson (translator). *The Magic of Minerals.* New York: Springer Verlag, 1986.

Willis, William. *The History of Portland.* Portland, ME: Maine Historical Society, 1972.

Wilson, Clarence G. *One God One Word.* Victoria, B.C., Canada: Trafford Publishing, 2004.

Wolfe, Amber. *Druid Power.* St. Paul, MN: Llewellyn Publications, 2005.

———. *Elemental Power.* St. Paul, MN: Llewellyn Publications, 2001.

Woodward, Fred. *Identifying Shells.* Secaucus, NJ: Chartwell Books, 1993.

Yogananda, Paramahansa. *Inner Peace: How to Be Calmly Active and Actively Calm.* Los Angeles: Self-Realization Fellowship, 1999.

INDEX